8 Tribes

8 Tribes

The hidden classes of New Zealand

Jill Caldwell & Christopher Brown

wicked little books
wellington

First Edition
2007

Wicked Little Books
PO Box 6838
Wellington

Copyright © Jill Caldwell and Christopher Brown 2007.
However, the authors acknowledge the role of well-intentioned piracy in the spread of all good ideas and encourage you to reproduce these pages and the ideas outlined on them for all purposes other than financial gain. If your intention is to reproduce any of the contents of this book for commercial purposes, we respectfully ask you not to be such a wanker and buy another copy of the book.

Jill Caldwell and Christopher Brown assert their moral rights to be identified as the authors of this work

ISBN-13: 978-0-473-11693-4

www.8tribes.co.nz

contents

1. The 8 Tribes of New Zealand   7
2. The North Shore Tribe   11
3. The Grey Lynn Tribe   25
4. The Balclutha Tribe   40
5. The Remuera Tribe   55
6. The Otara Tribe   69
7. The Raglan Tribe   83
8. The Cuba Street Tribe   96
9. The Papatoetoe Tribe   109
10. Your Tribal Profile   124
11. 8 Trends   126
12. 8 Tribes and the Future   148

— 1 —

The 8 Tribes of New Zealand

This is a book about the hidden classes of contemporary New Zealand. Class isn't a word people use often these days. It seems old fashioned and judgmental. It upsets our deep-seated notion of New Zealand as an egalitarian society. Researching this book, we found that most New Zealanders will do a lot to avoid using the word class to describe their relationship with others. But New Zealanders do recognise that there are some groups of people they identify with, and some they don't. They will talk at length about the differences in behaviour, the attitudes, even the dress that make them different from their embarrassing cousins or the schoolmates they've outgrown.

When you remove the overt references to hierarchy that class carries, New Zealanders embrace the idea of a society divided into different social identities. When we started calling the hidden classes of New Zealand our tribes, people were clamouring to see where they fitted in and why they found it so easy to decide that someone was "not my tribe".

Perhaps it's the same egalitarian spirit that makes us wary of words like class that makes us so receptive to the idea that there exists a "typical New Zealander", a person whose attitudes and lifestyle make up the archetype that defines us all. In our work in social research and marketing, we've encountered numerous attempts by corporate New Zealand to define this mythical creature over the years. Most often, these descriptions are collections of tired clichés about resourceful, hardworking, down-to-earth, friendly people, living in a clean, green world, swelling with pride as their compatriots regularly punch above their weight on the world stage.

We've found these experiences frustrating. Idealised views of the typical New Zealander don't offer any meaningful insights into what motivates people or touches their hearts. Ideas about the typical New Zealander encourage organisations to talk to people as if we were all the same, and result in communications that connect with no one and brands with little nuance or depth.

Our frustration with the myth of the typical New Zealander was what sparked the 8 Tribes project. Rather than look for what New Zealanders share in common with each other, we set out to explore how Kiwis see themselves as different from each other. We went searching for the distinctive social identities, the tribes of modern day New Zealand.

What we uncovered was a complex interplay of attitudes, values, prejudices and pretensions. We found eight distinctive social identities. These groupings aren't overt but most of them are instantly recognisable. In fact you can define them by the places where they're found in greater concentration — suburbs or towns.

The tribes we found might have a geography, but they cut across many other social boundaries. Financial, racial, age, gender, ethnic and occupational boundaries mean little to the tribal system. Most of the tribes are extremely diverse. It was especially surprising to find the minor role that money plays as a defining characteristic. It was, after all, the factor that underpinned old notions of the upper, middle and lower classes, but money really has a defining role in only two of the 8 Tribes — the North Shore tribe, where spending money is all-important in defining one's status, and the Remuera tribe, where an individual's connection to "old money" plays an important role in tribal acceptance.

The 8 Tribes system describes how people see themselves and identifies the signature attitudes that different groups of New Zealanders look for in others before they class them as "people like me". Each of the 8 Tribes is defined by a unique set of signature attitudes and distinctive lifestyle patterns.

These are the 8 Tribes:
- The North Shore tribe
- The Grey Lynn tribe
- The Balclutha tribe
- The Remuera tribe
- The Otara tribe
- The Raglan tribe
- The Cuba Street tribe
- The Papatoetoe tribe

The burning question is, where do you fit in?

− 2 −
The North Shore Tribe

Found in:
Suburbs of our biggest cities, commuting in cars to gather in gyms and at shopping malls.

Distinguishing Characteristics:
New cars, new toys, long commutes, tropical resort holidays, stress related health issues.

The North Shore tribe is populated by self-made men and women — self-starters with large doses of ambition, aspiration, perseverance and achievement. There's a simple and powerful philosophy underpinning this set of tribal values: you work out how the system operates, work hard, climb the ladder and enjoy the rewards at the top — the nice house, the nice car, the overseas holidays.

The North Shore tribe dominates many parts of New Zealand society, just as its counterparts do around the world. It's a core part of the "mainstream", the economically energetic class that drives our urban consumer economy and is so prized by our agenda-setting media networks and advertisers.

Money defines life for the North Shore tribe. It's the factor by which value judgments are made. Something is valuable or worthless according to its cost. Earning a decent income, striving to become comfortably wealthy and moving up the status ladder is the unquestioned point of life. Living in a way that expresses your success is natural. Your suburb, house, car, clothes and holidays all have status implications, and in the North Shore tribe, you should always go for the best your money can buy.

The Signature Attitudes of the North Shore Tribe

THE LAND OF OPPORTUNITY

"Anyone can achieve their potential if they work hard."

At the core of the North Shore tribe's mindset is a fundamental belief that with hard work and perseverance, anyone can achieve their potential.

This is an enormously optimistic and constructive attitude. Everyone has limitless potential — and there are loads of stories about state house-raised high-school dropouts becoming millionaires before they're 40 to prove it.

Achievement is measured by the ability to accumulate high-status possessions, job and lifestyle. Success is surrounding yourself with gorgeous stuff, having a high-powered career and accessing luxurious experiences.

The rewards might be luxurious, but getting there is not supposed to be easy. This attitude is a reworked Protestant work ethic for the consumer society — work hard, suffer a little, and get your heaven-on-earth right now. There's great admiration for late nights at the office, 60-hour weeks and a Robert the Bruce-like "try and try again" resilience. The key to achieving your potential is to work hard, focus on goals, take risks and persevere through setbacks.

The "virtue of work" attitude means that success brought about by luck is seen as secondary to that which is achieved through hard work. Inheriting millions might give you the trappings of success, but you'll always be second in estimation to the self-made man who created it all himself.

BEATING THE JONESES

"Life's a competition. You measure your level of success relative to the people around you."

In the 70s they called it "keeping up with the Joneses". But in the 21st century the gloves are off and it's all-out status war—winning is the goal that drives the North Shore tribe—to be richer, higher up the ladder at work, smarter, more fashionable, more influential and more beautiful than the people around them. Life is about beating your friends, enemies, family, classmates and neighbours by being more successful than they are.

The North Shore tribe is appalled when it sees the importance of winning undermined. There's a regular outcry when junior sports administrators suggest that participation on Saturday morning is more important than winning, or when the education system moves further away from measuring student achievement by ranking students in order from winners to losers.

The North Shore tribe loves to see New Zealand beat the world. The All Blacks, Team New Zealand, world-champion rowers and Peter Jackson are all loved because they've taken on the world and beaten it. Multiple Whitbread and America's Cup winner Peter Blake is eulogised as the patron saint of the North Shore tribe. Australians' hard-nosed competitive attitude is held in high regard in the North Shore tribe—"they know how to win those Aussies. If only we had more of that here".

THE SEXINESS OF STUFF

*"Life's too short to wear ugly clothes
and drink bad wine."*

The North Shore tribe is where the joy of consumerism reaches its apex.

North Shore tribe members genuinely adore gorgeous things and they love going out to find and buy them. They love giving the kids the kind of stuff they never had but always wanted, buying their wives or girlfriends beautiful jewellery or surprising husbands or boyfriends with some new toy they just have to have.

These are sensual people. They feel an exhilarating rush every time they sit down to watch a movie on their home theatre system or click on their new iPod Nano for the first time, or catch sight of the heels of their new Italian boots.

The North Shore tribe loves the pursuit of sexy new stuff. Shopping is a much-loved leisure activity and the thrill of making a fabulous new purchase or gaining access to a wonderful experience is profound. Tribe members love the feeling of getting dressed up for a smart party, or playing a round on an international-standard golf course. The sexiness of stuff offers reason for being.

The flipside is a sense of genuine privation when new stuff and luxury is denied. If the household belt needs tightening and there's less money for shopping, members of the North Shore tribe are likely to become agitated quickly. They'll feel like their life is missing something. Soon they'll graduate to a genuine sense of grievance. But relief is only one good blow-out on the credit card away.

THE FEAR OF STANDING STILL

*"If you're not going forwards
you're going backwards."*

There is no such thing as standing still in the North Shore tribe. This is the tribe of progress, of social mobility. In this tribe, things that stand still rust and decay. Fashions change by the season. Old cars need replacing with shiny new ones. You get sick of your house after a while.

If members of the North Shore tribe aren't moving up, they fret. If they're not constantly engaged in the cycle of reinvention through consumption, they worry about sliding backwards down the ladder of achievement.

For many, the motivation for this is basic financial survival. North Shore tribal lifestyles are expensive and many require high levels of debt servicing. Without the cash income, the symbols of success disappear, and the unthinkable happens — you lose, beaten by the Joneses.

The prospect is appalling. It took years to get to this position; going backwards would mean all those years were wasted. How could you go back to a tired Honda from a peppy late model Audi? What would people say?

To counter this fear, members of the North Shore tribe crave the financial security that would allow them to continue their high-consuming lifestyle even without work. They look for it in many places — insurances, investments, even Lotto, though they'd probably never admit they'd won.

Fear of Standing Still is at the root of what many people from other tribes deride as workaholism. If someone has so much, why do they need to keep working so hard? Because they don't see that they have a lot. No matter how much they have, they see that as just enough.

KNOW THE RULES BEST

*"You can tell a lot about a person
from how they live."*

To the highly competitive mind of the North Shore tribe, the world is a strict status hierarchy. Your purpose in life is to position yourself as high up that hierarchy as possible. You do that through the lifestyle you create — where you live, where you work, what you wear, what you drive, where you holiday, how much money you spend, your celebrity.

In every area of endeavour, there are rules to master and a pecking order to understand. It's a complex and subtle game of lifestyle semiotics. The importance of knowing rules is most obvious in the world of fashion. All the tribes follow fashion to some extent, but for the North Shore tribe it's fundamental. Buying the right shoes for the season is as much of a necessity as grocery shopping.

There's a status list for every area of consumption and lifestyle. Your suburb, your interior, your car, your holiday, your kids' schools, even your kids' names. The high priests and priestesses of the North Shore tribe mark their place by their mastery of these status hierarchies. They have the money to buy the expensive options, but they don't just buy what's in the glossy magazines—they've mastered the art of knowing what will be the next big thing. The less successful members of the tribe note their choices, and follow their lead.

The Lifestyle of the North Shore Tribe

Work

Work is at the heart of life in the North Shore tribe. It provides not only the essential income for tribal membership, but also status, fulfilment and structure. For many in the North Shore tribe, their work is a fundamental part of who they are.

You mostly find North Shore tribe members in managerial roles or in their own businesses. They are the entrepreneurs with the solid business plans, not the flaky dreams. They're the commission salespeople who really know how to sell. Or the highly motivated workers who put in the big hours and aim for the big bonuses. These are the deal-makers, the "can-do Kiwis" who make things happen. You find them in roles which exist to finance, develop, build, organise and sell the products of consumer society.

Members of the North Shore tribe tend to be ambitious in the workplace, always looking move up, always up for a pay rise, always looking to be more important. They tend not to stay with one employer too long. Unless they're still moving up, they'll move on. Being head-hunted to a more prestigious, better-paying job is the ultimate buzz. And these are the people who will network their butts off to make sure those calls are made to them.

Leisure

The North Shore tribe lives for its holidays. Overseas holidays are especially important because they carry status value as well as being a respite from hard work. Working late for weeks to clear away work for the winter family holiday at a Fijian resort is a traditional North Shore tribal ritual.

Overseas destinations have a strict status hierarchy too — starting with the "wardrobe basics" of weekends in Sydney and condos at Noosa, and culminating in the latest exotic destination — Cuba, the islands of Croatia, safari in Africa: the choices are limitless and presented beautifully in travel sections of glossy magazines.

Time and convenience are very important to the North Shore tribe. Inefficient leisure is a sin. Multi-tasking and streamlining your way of life are obvious strategies. You maximise leisure time by contracting out anything that doesn't really make good use of your skills, like ironing and weeding the garden.

That leaves more time for the important things. For women, shopping is the number one leisure activity, closely followed by "appearance leisure" — visits to gyms, day spas and hair salons all count as leisure. And if anyone's keeping himself in shape, it's the male of the North Shore tribe. He has no intention of giving up his advantage to younger guys. He'll still be beating them at squash when he's 50. He works long hours and outside holidays and weekends, doesn't have much time for leisure. Perhaps the most common image of masculine leisure in the North Shore tribe is Man Alone, late home from the office, watching sport by himself on a very large television.

Money

Money is the most important thing in the North Shore tribal world. It's the key to progress and the font of all things good—gorgeous things, experiences, status and security.

Financial planning is important. Having the money to help your children access all the opportunities possible is among a parent's prime responsibilities. The rules of compound interest are well understood in the North Shore tribe.

In the North Shore tribe's perfect scenario, everything is mapped out: income, insurances, investments. But life doesn't always follow the script. It's more likely that a typical member of the North Shore tribe lives his or her life with an angel on one shoulder whispering "plan and save" and a devil on the other screaming "spend—you deserve that sexy new car NOW!"

Home

The home is central to the North Shore tribe. Their priority is a good address—somewhere that's safe for the family, in good school zones and, very importantly, in an area with a good name.

This isn't a tribe that sets a lot of store by staying in the same place for ever and a day. Instead, they map a trajectory of more-or-less continual upwards movement — from starter suburb to safe suburb and then on to smart suburb. Their homes follow a similar path — from worst house in a good street to best house in a great street.

For most in this tribe, the home is the primary investment vehicle for getting ahead. Home improvement for capital gain is often a passion. Many of them turn over houses regularly — moving in, doing a makeover, making a good sale and moving on. House prices are a favourite topic of conversation. Property investments suit their preference for tangible wealth.

– 3 –
The Grey Lynn Tribe

Found in:
Suddenly fashionable ex-working class suburbs.
Large groups will gather at bohemian inner city cafes,
intellectual bookshops, ethnic cultural events and
film festivals.

Distinguishing Characteristics:
Prefers to be "challenged" than entertained,
seeks out authentic experiences, blushes when talking
about property values.

The Grey Lynn tribe is made up of intellectuals who value ideas more than things. They are well-educated, highly principled, socially aware, culturally sophisticated people. They believe in collective social responsibility, and that individuals should make a difference by making the world a better place.

This growing tribe is increasingly influential within New Zealand. It might not control the big business decisions, but it is ascendant in government—both Parliament and the Public Service are Grey Lynn tribe dominated institutions. In the private sector, Grey Lynn tribe members are often educators or work in the creative industries.

The Grey Lynn tribe is made up of relatively affluent people with high-paying knowledge-worker jobs. Affluence allows them to live in comfort and to access things they love—art, travel, a vibrant social life, well-made things. But it's sometimes hard to reconcile your level of affluence with your principles—having so much when the world is a mess. The Grey Lynn tribe's solution is to seek out authenticity and to craft a life that makes a difference.

The Signature Attitudes of the Grey Lynn Tribe

A THEORY FOR EVERY ACTION

"I think, therefore I am."

If New Zealand has an intelligentsia, the Grey Lynn tribe would like to think that it is it. They are university-trained people who find ideas stimulating and fulfilling. They regard the opinions you hold as a direct reflection of your intellect, which in turn measures your worth as a person. They've taken Descartes at his word and formed their identities around their capacity for abstract thought.

In the Grey Lynn tribe there's nothing better than a knotty intellectual problem to discuss. Their preferred entertainment is a mental challenge—film, literature and other art-forms that stimulate their thinking, rather than simply amusing or moving them emotionally. These are the book buyers, the readers of "serious" magazines and literature, the theatre and film festival-goers. They worry about the "dumbing down" of the media.

When the Grey Lynn tribe gets materialistic, it becomes an intellectual exercise. Objects with the most intellectual significance are the most precious. A designer piece of furniture is valued not for its comfort, but for its "significance". Books are treasured as an extension of one's mind. "Challenging" art is admired; anything "merely decorative" is scoffed at.

Intellectualism has become the religion of the Grey Lynn tribe. When they need comfort, they turn to their minds. They intellectualise their emotional issues, rationalise their sticky situations and make plans to sort it out. When they encounter something new and disturbing, they read a book about it, watch a documentary or look it up in Wikipedia.

For members of the Grey Lynn tribe, knowledge is the font of all goodness, ignorance the cause of evil. They believe that education has the power to make the world a better place by improving each individual. And every individual has the desire to become better through exposure to education — as Oprah Winifrey puts it "when you knew better, you did better".

That's why they believe in social marketing. If you explain your reasons clearly, people will automatically do the right thing. The Grey Lynn tribe would, anyway.

THE COLLECTIVE GOOD

"It's your responsibility to accept that what's best for the group is best for each individual."

Scratch the surface of a Grey Lynn tribe member and you'll detect a strong socialist urge — a belief that what's best for the group is best for the individual. The typical Grey Lynn tribe member doesn't begrudge paying tax and genuinely believes in the public education system and the public health system. They dream of the time when New Zealand's social infrastructure was the best in the world.

Belief in the collective good puts the Grey Lynn tribe at the opposite end of the political spectrum from libertarians, who champion the individual's right to chose, wise markets, small governments and low taxes. The Grey Lynn tribe sees it as the government's role to wield a judicious intervening hand into social and economic affairs. The government is responsible for protecting society's weak through policing working standards and providing benefit payments, free healthcare and education. The government is responsible for solving social issues through legislation, education programmes and social marketing campaigns.

In their own communities, belief in the collective good can leave Grey Lynn tribe members with conflicting desires. On one hand, Grey Lynn is the tribe of shared community experiences and facilities — of toy libraries, street fairs and tree-planting projects. But on the other hand, the Grey Lynn tribe can also tend toward the well-meaning extremism of rules and more rules. This is the tribe that creates a wonderful playground experience and then stops the children using it because there's no safety plan in place.

WE CAN CHANGE THE WORLD

"By changing the way we each live our individual lives, we can change the world."

Grey Lynn tribe members tend to be committed and empowered people. They have a strong sense of duty to help to improve the world, and an equally strong sense of their own ability to make a difference. Put them together and you get the tribal urge for activism — the disposition toward action, no matter how small.

Grey Lynn tribe members have no shortage of causes to support. They are far more sensitised to fighting injustice than other tribes. It's the Grey Lynn tribe which understands best how politics and issues work, that sees the double-edged impact of marketing, the downside of globalisation and the significance of climate change. At the local level, it's the Grey Lynn tribe who can link these global issues to developments in their own community.

Time constraints mean the Grey Lynn tribe can't get involved in everything. To avoid compassion fatigue, members tend to commit themselves to a few special causes. These might be small actions (buying Fair Trade organic coffee, washing their cars on the grass so the suds don't go down the gutter into the ocean), or big (organising a mass campaign to stop a development on the local coastline). But whatever the scale of their expression, every Grey Lynn tribe member will always have a story about how his or her actions are helping to make the world a better place.

BEING COGNOSCENTI

"It's the significance of a thing that creates its value, not the price."

Knowledge is the ultimate currency in the Grey Lynn tribe. Knowledge is obtained through experiencing, reading, discussing or knowing connected people. Being cognoscenti—the ones who know—is central to achieving status in the Grey Lynn tribe.

Inside knowledge gives you the greatest status, especially if it was acquired long before anyone else recognised its significance. That's ultimate proof that you are smart and connected—you understood before the rabble did. You get boosted status in Grey Lynn if you can show that you were recycling in 1982 or had a website in 1995.

Status is not directly conferred by money or possessions, but by objects that tell the story of your sensitivity or your prescience. How an object came into your possession is often central to its status value. Having an art work by a rising contemporary New Zealand "it" artist is highly prestigious—a big Shane Cotton painting will do nicely. But to have bought it last week for $100,000 will not give you Grey Lynn tribal status. Status comes from showing you were in the know before the herd. Perhaps you paid $10,000 at an early show? Or better still, you were given it by the artist as thanks for something meaningful you did to help him on the way up.

THERE ARE NO SHORTCUTS TO AUTHENTICITY

"The best things in life are a test of your commitment."

In the Grey Lynn tribe, the real thing is always better than a reproduction. Even if the reproduction is functionally better, it doesn't have the innate value of the original.

This attitude comes partly from the value placed on insider knowledge within the Grey Lynn tribe, but it also has origins in the Calvinist hair-shirt — the sense that there is virtue in suffering. For members of the Grey Lynn tribe, suffering and authenticity are closely linked.

The novel written by the obscure, poor writer in a freezing flat has more authenticity, and hence artistic value, than the "commercial" alternative, loved by the masses, but written in comfort by the warm author with a million-dollar advance. If that garret-written novel happens to be plot-less, esoteric, and written with Joyce-like disregard for the conventions of English grammar, then its value as a status object rises exponentially.

The same is true of experiences. Watching an obscure sub-titled film festival movie — hard work on both the eyes and the brain — is intrinsically better than the experience of being spoon fed a Hollywood blockbuster. Grimy backpack travel among the peasants in the Third World is a far more virtuous holiday than sipping cocktails beside the pool on Denarau Island.

The Lifestyle of the Grey Lynn Tribe

Work

The Grey Lynn tribe is the heart of the creative classes. Members tend to steer clear of work that returns only a monetary reward in favour of jobs that are meaningful or imaginative. They have very committed and busy lives. This is New Zealand's intellectual tribe so it's not surprising that most of their careers involve mental rather than physical work.

In the past two decades this kind of work has grown significantly, especially in the private sector. Control by number crunchers, accountants and engineers is waning, and as it does, the value of creativity, design and communication is rising—the "value-added" work of the Grey Lynn tribe.

Grey Lynn tribe members are involved in areas where they can create social improvement, such as government departments, universities and polytechnics. Their preference is for research, communications or policy positions, though you also find them leading, administering and gate-keeping.

They also populate the not-for-profit sector. Greatest intellectual rigour may be found in organisations like Greenpeace, Forest and Bird or Amnesty International, but there is something very satisfying to a Grey Lynn tribe member about facilitating the needs of any good cause.

Leisure

The venue of choice for the Grey Lynn tribe is the café — to a large extent they are "café society" and the neighbourhoods they congregate in reflect this, with their European ambience and strong street presence. Despite their busy lives, the Grey Lynn tribe members love to talk.

This tribe supports a wide range of cultural expression — theatre, art, music, film — because they're continually seeking intellectual stimulation. Being interesting is very important to them, and cultural experience makes you more interesting in their terms.

There's a strong preference for outdoor sports you can do with friends: tramping, sea kayaking, rock climbing and mountain biking are all favoured by the Grey Lynn tribe. Something elemental, not too much technology, nor too much cost. Test cricket is a favourite game and often even rugby, when it's played well.

The Grey Lynn tribe wants to be enlightened and at one with the world. Members improve their minds by reading literature and well-written magazines. There's also a lot of wellbeing recovery going on for these tired, busy people. Music, yoga, and meditation are common.

Participating in and contributing to their communities is a very high-value leisure activity for Grey Lynn tribe members. They believe in giving something back — whether it's volunteering at the toy library, cleaning up the foreshore, or running a stall at the local school fair. If anyone's on first-name terms with the teachers at their kid's school it will be someone from the Grey Lynn tribe.

Money

The Grey Lynn tribe really doesn't set out to become rich. Wealth just happens as tribe members live their lives — their homes rise in value, their skills turn out to be in demand. But they just want to be comfortable, to travel well and to give their children the things they'll need for life in an unknowable future. There's a desire to be responsible and to plan for the things you can anticipate, like retirement and children going to university. This tribe donates to charity, sponsors Third World children and supports worthy causes.

Though just as prone to hedonism as anyone else, Grey Lynn tribal members are often quite sensible with money, controlling their own purse strings and being careful to put money away for longer-term projects like travel and home ownership. The last thing a Grey Lynn tribe member wants to own up to is a maxed-out credit card. That's just playing into the hands of the multi-nationals. But these things do happen. They like to buy clothes that will last and cars that won't depreciate too fast, and as they rise in income, they tend to subscribe to the notion that quality costs money.

Home

The homes of the Grey Lynn tribe are a deliberate explanation of the owners' personal aesthetics. Typically, there is a desire to preserve the loveliest aspects of the heritage villa, pioneer cottage or modernist icon. Essential home accessories include paintings by children (whether or not children live in this home), wooden floors and/or leadlight windows, and tapa cloth or an authentic Maori craft piece. In the pantry there will be herbal teas and organic ingredients.

Because they have little interest in social climbing through housing, tribe members may have initially bought a quite modest home in a reasonable suburb — maybe an apartment in the city or a rustic little cottage. But like attracts like, so they begin to congregate together, drawn by the common elements of safety, charming cafés and leafy trees.

Homes once rented to poor people are bought and done up by middle-class people. House values rise and the Grey Lynn tribe begins to indulge in shame-faced conversations about property values. The negative consequences of these changes for the previous inhabitants, who now must live further out of the city or save much more to buy such a house, are carefully skirted.

– 4 –
The Balclutha Tribe

Found in:
Towns with a single main street and muddy utes.
Gathers in clubrooms, memorial halls and at the
Cossie Club.

Distinguishing Characteristics:
Down-to-earthness, talks of weather, moans about the
government.

THE BALCLUTHA TRIBE

The Balclutha tribe is New Zealand's heartland tribe, populated by down-to-earth, practical, conservative people from the provinces. If you ask New Zealander about the "typical kiwi", chances are they'll describe Balclutha tribal characteristics—hard-working, understated, resourceful, hospitable, deceptively smart.

The Balclutha tribe has a strong hold on our self-image as Kiwis. Balclutha tribal archetypes dominate the picture our culture makers feed to us of New Zealanders. The strong, humble All Black archetype is pure Balclutha. Our most famous advertising stories are Balclutha stories: the Speights shepherds, the Mainland cheese old blokes, and Toyota's "bugger"-cursing farmer.

It's a can-do, self-reliant tribe. Members of the Balclutha tribe, male and female, are expected to be resilient and tough; making do with what they've got and solving their own problems, hard working and never flashy.

These are people who have a stronger sense of both the past and the landscape than do many city dwellers. They live in areas that don't change so much, that are more geographically separated. They have a greater sense of being part of a community and in touch with their neighbours, and a stronger sense of how things used to be.

The Signature Attitudes of the Balclutha Tribe

CLOSE BUT NOT CLOSED

"We love different new people — as long as they're not weirdos."

Community plays a central role in the Balclutha tribal life, not surprising for a tribe with a direct lineage back to the land. When found in their native rural and small town setting, community life is all encompassing — they play on the same sports teams, go to the same weddings and funerals or tangi, belong to the same clubs, turn up to the same events. Several generations of the same family often live in close proximity, working or socialising together.

This makes them a close group, but they're not closed. New people will be warmly welcomed and embraced by the community as long as they prove they conform to Balclutha tribe attitudes. On the other hand, if you show too much deviation from the norm, you risk being rejected for being "up yourself" or just plain unusual.

When the Balclutha tribe finds itself in the city, this "close but not closed" sense of community remains important. Tribe members place great significance on their networks of old friends, on the longevity of relationships, and on the trust that knowing someone for a long time generates. In business, the Balclutha tribe tends to cultivate enduring business relationships with people they've known for a long time. Often the line between business associates and friends is blurred.

Introductions count for a lot in the Balclutha tribe. With the right endorsement, you'll be embraced quickly by a tribe member. If you're doing business with a member of the Balclutha tribe, the "who do you know?" and "where are you from?" ritual can be vital. When you play out this ritual with the Remuera tribe, it's a test for how posh you are. With the Balclutha tribe, it's a test of your trustworthiness. Show that you're close to an old friend from their inner network and they'll trust you immediately.

GET STUCK IN

*"Good people aren't afraid of a
bit of hard work."*

The Balclutha tribe has a profound work ethic. Hard physical work is not a necessary evil, it's a virtuous thing to be embraced. A person with a voracious appetite for hard work is highly admirable; a person without hard work, is inferior.

The rural roots of the Balclutha tribe are seen clearly in this attitude. The Kiwi farmer feels the heritage of hard work that built the farm up from nothing—it wasn't many generations ago that the bush was being cleared to make the farm. Seasonal farm tasks are arduous and long, but the exhausted satisfaction from completing a hard day's work on the farm is hard to match.

In the Balclutha tribe, workers are expected to be resourceful, highly motivated and to have the common sense to do what needs to be done. This is not a tribe for procrastinators or excuse-makers. In the Balclutha tribe, when a job needs to be done, you get stuck in and do it. If someone else has a lot on, you get stuck in and help them.

You get some points for turning up, but this is this get-the-job-done tribe, and you get most points for how much of the job you complete. You get no points for standing around waiting to be told what to do.

Balclutha tribe CEOs are the most likely to be found on the factory floor, driving a truck or wielding a shovel to prove to their workers that they're not afraid of "real" hard work.

This attitude breeds the "capable women" that have such a defining impact on New Zealand society. For generations, farmer's wives and daughters have been expected to manage the domestic front, but also get stuck in on the farm when necessary — bake a pav, shoot a rabbit and flip a sheep in the sheds to help with crutching. With this cultural heritage, it's hardly surprising that our first two female Prime Ministers were a farmer's wife and a farmer's daughter.

KEEP YOUR HEAD DOWN

"People who shout about how good they are are heading for a fall."

Tall poppies don't grow in a Balclutha tribal garden. It's a tribe where you keep your head down and don't get above of yourself. That's not to say it's a tribe of mediocrity. The Balclutha tribe is highly achievement oriented; but in this tribe you are quietly successful, not flashy.

There's a strong awareness that "pride comes before a fall" and understatement is the safety mechanism used to guard against that fall. Understatement is the key tool that allows you to celebrate individual skills and successes. "We did alright," describes winning a championship. "It's going OK," refers to a runaway business success. "Well George, we knocked the bastard off," describes becoming the first man to climb Mount Everest.

Even the humour is understated in the Balclutha tribe. Straight-faced practical jokes are treasured, particularly when they're perpetrated on unsuspecting townies. Iconic rural TV show Country Calendar has continued this tradition over the years with a series of practical joke episodes. One of these, the classic show featuring a farming couple performing a symphony for their neighbours on their strained wire fence, has even made it into Te Papa.

This enthusiasm for creating the victims of practical jokes reveals the strong current of schadenfreude—glee at others' misfortune—that runs through the Balclutha tribal mind. There's nothing like seeing someone who's got above themselves being taken down a peg or two.

This is a tribe where you keep your head down, or you end up with everyone you know laughing at you.

NUMBER 8 WIRE

"There's no problem that a bit of Kiwi ingenuity can't fix."

No discussion of the heartland New Zealand tribe would be complete without mention of its most celebrated attitude—the number-8-wire mentality. This is the no-frills, no-fuss, no-problem-unsolvable attitude of a hardworking practical man or woman. It's a mechanism for getting around obstacles; if something breaks, fix it and get back to what you were doing in the first place. If your tool doesn't quite fit the job, make a new one that fits out of whatever you have lying about.

Essential to this attitude is a strong sense of function over form. The number-8-wire mentality has seldom produced a beautiful thing, but it has produced plenty of stories of against-the-odds achievement. The Bert Munro story from the movie "World's Fastest Indian" is pure number 8 wire — an ugly motorbike, but a fast one.

This disregard for form has led to the number-8-wire mentality being maligned by the design-lead "gurus" of recent years, who insist that form and function must co-exist in the modern world. But they are missing the point. Number 8 wire is an attitude that combines ingenuity with dogged determination. It's about always being capable, never making a drama out of a crisis, bringing a never-say-can't spirit to problem solving. The Balclutha tribe member with a fully developed number-8-wire mentality is never defeated by any problem.

TAKE THE LONG VIEW
"If it ain't broke, don't fix it."

The Balclutha tribe is conservative by nature. Tribe members are annoyed by change for the sake of change, preferring to see a rational reason behind any alteration of the status quo.

Balclutha tribe children are more likely to live a similar life to their parents than are the children of many other tribes. Many see their lives laid out in front of them — especially those who inherit family properties or businesses. You carry on what your parents began; you'll make your own improvements, put your own mark on it, and at the end of that you'll hand it on to the next generation. Of course the next generation may have its own ideas about whether it is prepared to take on the mantle, but that's a battle for the future.

The long view of the Balclutha tribe means that it's important for most tribe members to know where they come from; not just where they grew up, but their genealogical origins too. They're also likely to have a strong sense of affinity with a certain piece of land somewhere around New Zealand, even if they live in the city.

These two things, genealogy and acute sense of place,

are articulated most powerfully by the Balclutha tribe's Maori members. Increasing awareness of Maori cultural values by Pakeha in the Balclutha tribe has them beginning to see the relevance of whakapapa and turangawaewae in their own lives.

The Lifestyle of the Balclutha Tribe

Work

One of the distinctive facets of the Balclutha tribe's working life is the high proportion of owner-operators and contractors. Partly it's because you can — the web of relationships in provincial communities provides quite stable long-term working arrangements. But partly it's because you have to — there's a limited pool of permanent full-time jobs.

On the plus side, many provincial jobs offer a greater-than-usual amount of autonomy compared to that found in a city job with a similar skill set. A boss breathing down their necks, telling them what to do next is not something Balclutha tribe members particularly enjoy.

There's no doubt that there's often a more personal interest taken in customers by some of the Balclutha tribe's businesses than you would see in metropolitan areas. Sometimes, there's also a lack of urgency which other tribes find frustrating. The pace of life is definitely slower. But despite what the cheese ads portray, this tribe typically works to world-class standards of hygiene and efficiency — looking for any advantage they can get in terms of costs and speed.

Long hours are standard for business owners and workers alike. Shift workers in the processing plants often work 12 to 15-hour shifts — though not every day. But seasonality and variety are also standard. Very few workers do the same job day-in, day-out throughout the year. You have to be a bit of a Jack-of-all-trades to make a good living, especially when so much of the work is seasonal.

Leisure

When he's not working, a man from the Balclutha tribe might get away to spend time outdoors doing something he loves—traditional team sports, especially rugby, or hunter-gatherer activities like fishing or hunting. Balclutha tribe men like the outdoors, especially if there's some machinery and mud involved. Rally cars and dirt bikes are a strong part of their repertoire. But they sneer at the 4WD that only ever goes off-road by accident.

The women of the Balclutha tribe are more likely to play a team sport like netball or hockey. There's a lot of home-making activity, keeping their large gardens under control, and a lot of driving.

While longstanding friendships make socialising easy, they can lead to insularity. Newcomers to a Balclutha tribal area can still feel their newness for a lot longer than their more nomadic city counterparts might. But if you seem to be made of the right stuff and you make an effort to fit in, you'll be welcomed—bonus if you're a good rugby or netball player, or a hot chick.

Money

There's a feast-and-famine aspect to the small-business world of the Balclutha tribe. A good season and good commodity prices energise an entire community, but there's no expectation they'll last. The money you can earn at the works during the season is far greater than what you expect to make in the off-season.

So you learn to make hay while the sun shines. Rural supply firms and electrical stores suddenly burst with flash new equipment, vacant shops on the main street disappear overnight, all because the Balclutha tribe is having a good year. Maybe you're putting something away; more likely you're paying off accumulated debt and preparing to take on some more. It almost goes without saying that a good year on the farm puts land values up — even if the return on investment is actually almost static, you can never have too much land.

There's no doubt that incomes are lower in provincial areas, and if you lose one job it's often far harder to get another than it might be in a larger place. You might end up doing two or three jobs if you really want to get ahead. But on the other hand, your money goes a lot further in some ways — especially the cost of houses.

And as long as you don't work on the land you might get to have a real weekend.

Home

Balclutha tribe homes tend to be designed for function and comfort rather than style. There will be few frivolous extras, but there will be a very cost-effective version of all the modern home's necessities. Good modern kitchen, bathroom and the big TV and La-Z-Boy in the living room. Balclutha tribe members stay in a lot.

When they're in the country, Balclutha tribe homes are often larger and older than are their city counterparts. They have big sections — gardening isn't an optional extra, and it's often performed according to the "get stuck in" attitude. It's not uncommon for gardens to be large and labour intensive. The Balclutha tribe is the last bastion of the "couple of rows of spuds" school of vege gardening.

City people find the country people's attitude to home security a little alarming. "You have to say to them: lock your car, lock the door!" Despite the rise of rural crime, you're still far more likely to find doors of this tribe unlocked.

– 5 –

The Remuera Tribe

Found in:
Leafy enclaves of the elite old city suburbs and in leafy corners of provincial towns with old sheep-grazier traditions

Distinguishing Characteristics:
Rounded vowels, meticulous manners.

The Remuera tribe is New Zealand's self-declared upper class, people with an acute awareness of a social hierarchy and an untroubled sense of entitlement to a place at its top. Like the class-obsessed English culture it emulates, the Remuera tribe works hard to preserve its position of privilege. Central to this process is a life lived to strict set of social rules and behaviours through which one declares belonging to the Remuera tribe.

The modern world hasn't been overly kind to the Remuera tribe, and numbers of the pure Remuera tribal strain are dwindling. Control of the corporate world and bureaucracy have been ceded to the North Shore and Grey Lynn tribes. But even though many pure-bred Remuera tribe children grow up and join the North Shore, Grey Lynn or Raglan tribes, most still show their roots with manners and affectations they just can't bring themselves to shake off.

Affluence is at the base of this tribe, and like its English model, it values old money highest. Just getting rich won't buy you entrance into the Remuera tribe. First, there's a complex social dance to learn. Then there's a good generation of living-by-the-rules before you can truly join the Establishment.

The Signature Attitudes of the Remuera Tribe

PEDIGREE

"Who was your mother?"

The Remuera tribe's elitist worldview values breeding over all else. Money will buy you a lot of status, but without a good pedigree you'll always be a little arriviste, no matter how hard you try. Of course, your kids won't have the same problem. Keep the wealth in the family for a couple of generations and it becomes that most well-bred of all things, old money.

Nothing indicates pedigree more than old money. In this tribe, the age of your fortune can even make up for deficiencies in its size. A complex status equation balances the age and mass of your money to decide exactly where you fit in the greater scheme of things.

But not everyone in this tribe has old money. For these strugglers there are rules of pedigree:

– Your parents (better still, your grandparents too) went to the same private school as you did, and

you can prove continuous occupation through multiple generations in a big house in a posh suburb.
- Your ancestors have been in New Zealand from early European settlement and you have ancestral links to the English aristocracy (it's not necessary to prove these).
- Somewhere in the past your family become fabulously wealthy from its daring undertakings in the colonial economy. The faintest vestiges of this old money linger.
- There is a street, or better still, a lane, named after your ancestor in a posh suburb of your town.

GENTEEL MANNERS

"You must know how to behave in public."

There's a strict behavioural code you must adhere to in the Remuera tribe that covers how you act and how you talk. When you follow the code, you signal to other members of the Remuera tribe that you're of the tribe.

Central to the code of behaviour are old-fashioned good manners, a reflex for the Remuera tribe and a core mechanism for identifying other Remuera tribe members. Behaviour that could appear as anachronistic, affected and effete to another tribe is a sign of breeding for this tribe. Males consider themselves chivalric toward women — holding doors and standing when a woman enters the room. Mealtimes are refined affairs and social encounters are filled with balanced, considerate conversations.

Dialect is very important. The Remuera tribal dialect is a round-vowelled attempt to identify itself more closely with the English Home Counties and to set itself apart from the "vernacular" New Zealand accent. There are vocabulary rules as well. In the Remuera tribe, one relieves oneself in the loo or lavatory, never the toilet. One uses a table napkin not a serviette while eating dinner, not tea.

Of course, there are exceptions. Like the eccentric bohemian fringe of the English aristocracy, the Remuera tribe treasures the few members of its elite sub-tribe, the filthy-rich-old-moneyed-idle, who chose to flaunt these rules and live according to some other set of values. Breeding and old money will forgive many sins in the Remuera tribe.

THE RIGHT KIND OF PEOPLE
"Where did you go to school?"

At the core of the Remuera tribe is a sense that it constitutes a superior social caste. Consequently, the natural instinct of a Remuera tribe member is to seek out other members of the Remuera tribe.

This means Remuera tribal society is highly networked in complex webs of friendship and acquaintance between the right kind of people. Many of these networks are formed at the country's elite private schools and are maintained through adult life, as the children of privilege disperse to the far corners of the country to populate the appropriate suburbs.

These networks are often very geographically dispersed. Socially active members of the Remuera tribe will spend several weekends a year at parties with old friends around the country. Through the years, different Remuera tribal social networks intersect and cross-pollinate. It's not uncommon for them to extend out beyond single generations and for family friends to become quasi-relations.

Belonging to one Remuera tribe social network becomes an introduction to others. "Do you know..." is never a casual question when uttered by someone from the Remuera tribe.

RIGHTFULLY ABOVE
"Luck has nothing to do with it."

Members of the Remuera tribe sleep easily with the knowledge of their position at the apex of society, sure in their sense of rightful privilege. Society is naturally hierarchical and there is always a group that rises to the top. A person of the Remuera tribe is unlikely to perceive the fact that he or she belongs to an elite group as lucky anymore than a cat might consider being born a cat a stroke of luck. "It's the natural order, and this is where

I fall in it." A child of privilege naturally sees his or her privilege as the natural order.

It's natural in the Remuera tribe to expect a better-than-average run at education, healthcare and the most lucrative professions. That's not to say children of the Remuera tribe don't work hard or display talent to achieve at an elite level, just that they are comfortable that this is the natural way of things for people from their background.

Though we think of this as a white tribe, there are many high-status Maori with strong Remuera tribe connections. The mutual ease with elitism creates a natural affinity. It's hardly surprising that the first Treaty of Waitangi settlement process was kick-started by a son of the Remuera tribe, Sir Douglas Graham, or that the first settlement was signed by the Maori Queen.

Belief in privileged status runs deep. A Remuera tribe member with limited genetic abilities and a family fortune washed away by the years is likely to harbour a deep sense of injustice that pedigree doesn't bestow material reward.

THE GREATER GOOD

"One does what one can."

The inverse of entitlement is the Remuera tribe's sense of obligation to contribute to the world in some way as the duty of privilege. It's the impulse of the philanthropist—a mix of genuine compassion with a desire for status through recognition of largesse.

This attitude isn't to be confused with the Grey Lynn tribe's egalitarian impulses for good works. Rather, it's a patrician instinct of noblesse oblige, the ultimate expression of a rightful place at the head of society's ruling caste.

This attitude manifests in many ways. Sometimes you see it subtly—as a well-formed and forcefully delivered opinion on changes to the local community. Sometimes it's more obvious—the calling to public office or charity work; leading the company to develop its sense of corporate responsibility; or taking a lead role in a local project aiming to leave lasting legacy for the local community.

One of the most striking examples of this attitude in action in New Zealand has been the philanthropic dedication of the McKenzie family—headed most recently by Sir Roy Mackenzie ONZ. Sir Roy, the McKenzie department store heir, spent years devoted fulltime to philanthropic works, initially via his father's JR McKenzie Trust and later through vehicles Sir Roy established himself—the Roy McKenzie Foundation and the McKenzie Education Foundation.

The Lifestyle of the Remuera Tribe

Work

You're most likely to find Remuera tribe members working for themselves as partners in professional firms or as shareholder-managers in other businesses. The Remuera tribe feels most comfortable when it doesn't have to call anyone boss—especially not someone from a lower caste.

The Remuera tribe shares the Kiwi hard work ethic, but in a slightly qualified way. Remuera tribe members admire people who work hard and work smart. Working hard for someone else for an hourly rate is seen as foolish. Working hard towards a performance-related bonus is smart. Working smart and embracing risk to further amplify the potential gains is the smartest yet. Where the Remuera tribe members are employees, it's likely to be in high-value sectors such as finance or some other area where big deals and big windfalls are common.

The Remuera tribe was once the embodiment of New Zealand's ruling class in every area. But with every post-colonial generation, its influence has fallen away. These days the Remuera tribe has ceded political and culture-making power to the Grey Lynn and North Shore tribes. But the Remuera tribe remains a powerful force in our society. It runs some of the most lucrative areas of the New Zealand economy like a round-vowelled secret society — our elite law firms, financial sector institutions, and the boardrooms of our largest corporations are all enclaves of Remuera tribe members, on the lookout for the next person-like-them to do business with.

Leisure

Leisure is something the Remuera tribe does well. Work smart, play lavishly might well be their leisure catch-cry. Holidays designed around expensive sports are common. Remuera tribe kids learn to ski or snowboard with their families in winter and to sail and wakeboard in summer.

Socialising occurs within strict rules of generosity and reciprocity. Dinner parties at one's house are undertaken according to the rules of genteel manners, one of which is reciprocity of hospitality. Remuera tribe members are commonly foodies, and the dinner party menu is likely to be exotic.

Foreign holidays avoid resorts, unless they are "exclusive". Remuera tribe members are more likely to be freedom travellers, staying in a hotel, shopping and exploring the posher places wherever they are.

Their houses tend to have large sections and established trees, so gardening is a popular activity. Well-tended lawns, trimmed buxus and hawthorn hedges, oak trees, English flower borders and roses are prominent features of the Remuera tribe garden.

Money

Although the Remuera tribe is seldom so crass as to speak openly of money in social settings, it is extremely important. Not all money is equal. The primary rule of money for the Remuera tribe is that old money is best.

Inheriting wealth is a great show of pedigree. If you're rich because your Granddad was, you have an automatic cachet.

Not that making money is looked down upon; it's a highly admired virtue. Remuera is an extremely entrepreneurial tribe and business prowess is highly regarded.

The combination of money-making nous and old money produces the Remuera tribe superhuman. Multigenerational trust fund kid Douglas Myers, who turned the family millions into hundreds of millions is a true Remuera tribe hero.

Within the caste, there are further fine gradations based on current wealth, and people move up or down the hierarchy all the time according to their financial fate. But the age of your money dictates the extent of your potential rise or fall. A deal-making maestro who happened to have begun life as a butcher's apprentice, such as Eric Watson, will never make the Remuera tribe's most-admired list. A less successful deal-maker who happens to be a scion of the establishment will be far better regarded for growing the family wealth and wheeling and dealing to build his own fortune.

Home

The Remuera tribe is a clustering group. You find its members in leafy enclaves — Remuera, Fendalton, Havelock North, Kelburn, Maori Hill. Traditionally, they were also common on big farms, although gentlemen farmers are an increasingly scarce breed after bad times in the 1980s saw the demise of the elite boarding-school tradition for many farmers' sons.

Address is extremely important to the Remuera tribe. Within each enclave, there will be a very strict view of the hierarchy of addresses — from the best address to those that are only just acceptable. Moving oneself outside this hierarchy of streets is social suicide for the Remuera tribe.

Remuera tribe homes are pictures of "good taste". Essentially that means a conservative, classical aesthetic. There will be two of everything: lamps, candelabras, paintings of horses. While the specifics of architectural styles and interior tastes might vary, most Remuera tribe homes will have at least one traditional element as a visible sign of pedigree — perhaps an heirloom antique side table filled with silver-framed family photos. A European car will be in the garage.

– 6 –
The Otara Tribe

Found in:
Areas with concentrations of churches and
state housing.

Distinguishing Characteristics:
Large social gatherings, infectious laughter, wearing of
flowers, men in skirts.

The Otara tribe is made up of ethnic minorities, often immigrants, whose lives centre on family and a community of people from the old countries or tribal areas.

It contains a broad spectrum of ethnic groups, many of which are Pacific Islanders or Maori from traditional backgrounds, but also includes people from other developing countries. Older people have told us that this tribal portrait could also apply to working class Pakeha Catholics of the previous generation. What unites the diverse ethnic groups of the Otara Tribe is their common quest to blend their traditional social values with those of the twenty-first century consumer society in which they now are embedded.

At its base there is a clear conflict between two quite different world views, between the traditional values of church, clan or village, and the materialist values of progress, acquisition and individuality. Money opens the door to far greater well-being for yourself and your family, but the costs of transition are many and subtle.

Life in the Otara tribe is about being part of a community and working to sustain that group. Community members celebrate the good times together and help each other out when times are tough. They congregate together at the beach, church, marae feast, market, or sports and cultural events. Status comes from family position and is expressed in your contribution to the community. Giving establishes your worth. Life is lived to a strong moral code, more often than not based on strong spiritual belief.

The Signature Attitudes of the Otara Tribe

BEING A PART

"You don't have to explain yourself to them."

The Otara tribe is the least individualistic of all the tribes. Here you are first and foremost part of a group — part of a family, a club, a church, or maybe a gang. Part of a community, part of a culture. A recognisable part.

It's not just a matter of what tribe members were brought up to do or who helped them out in the past, it's embedded in the whole way of thinking of the community. Family is what there is. Extended family. The people you are related to are a direct reflection of you — for better or for worse. Without them you're diminished and without you, they are less. In your community you're related to almost everyone, one way or another.

But because you're here in urban New Zealand in the 21st century, rather than back home, the difference between the things you are a part of and the things you don't feel part of is heightened. Outside of your own community comfort zone you feel your differences. Or if you forget them for a little while, the reactions and responses of others will remind you of them. Little things, from the way they pronounce your name to the way they seem not to understand things that are self-evident to you. It's about always having to explain yourself.

UNPREDICTABLE DANGERS

"You never know what's around the corner."

The Otara tribe lives with greater risk than most other New Zealanders: insecure financial arrangements, physical work that might easily injure them, more dangerous neighbourhoods and health risks that can undermine their quality of life.

Otara tribe members have little or no belief in their ability to make things different, so attempts to change are seen as futile. It's best to be grateful for what you've got and uncomplaining in the face of danger or infirmity. Life might not be great — money might be tight and your personal life might be unsatisfying or even violent, but what makes you think it might be any better somewhere else?

There's an unpredictability to this life which few other New Zealanders would find palatable. There are always things to go wrong and it's hard to anticipate what they'll be. But rather than worrying about what might happen or making plans to combat all the problems that might arise, the people of this tribe live in the present, and wait for whatever it is to arrive, knowing that they will cope, as they always have.

BLESSED ARE THE MEEK

"I told God I'd try not to do it any more ... sorry God."

In the Otara tribe, faith in a higher power almost goes without saying—God is greater than us and will look after us. Often this is quite a personal god who's actively watching over you—frowning when you transgress, proud when you do well, but ultimately forgiving of your human frailties because you are so much less than God.

Otara tribe members don't believe in their ability to shape their destiny or change the world—that's for God to do. They put their faith in prayer and their family and community, but they also have a great deal of tolerance of discomfort and disappointment.

You try to live a moral life, be a good loyal family member, support your church and be a giving member of the community. Being lost to God—through drug use or by setting yourself up as a rival authority to God—is seen as a perilous choice, one that will almost certainly invite more bad things into your life.

By contrast, being saved, returned to the church and to the family is seen as a great blessing. Typically, there is belief in redemption and forgiveness in the Otara tribe—even for horrendous crime.

RESPECT, SHAME AND AUTHORITY

"He gave me a hiding for being caught smoking, but he smoked himself."

The thing about village life is that everybody's watching. If you have a certain status, through your age, your lineage or your family's achievements, there's a lot of mana or face to lose. Being shown to be less than you are expected to be is a highly shameful process. When it's your spouse or your child who causes such embarrassment, you feel both shame and anger.

Children of the Otara tribe almost all have stories of the hidings they got for causing shame to their family. It can lead to a finely tuned sense of hypocrisy if the shameful behaviours were learned at home, but it takes a lot to convince yourself that you didn't somehow deserve to be beaten.

In a country where the major urban tribes accord status to each other on the basis of merit or income rather than birth, it is difficult for members of the Otara tribe to get the respect they're traditionally entitled to as a result of their age, or their position in a traditional family or group. As migrants from less wealthy backgrounds they are almost inevitably seen as inferior to wealthier or whiter locals. There's tension in relationships with authority. Police and other officials are also often seen as interfering in the lives of Otara tribe members, not respecting them, and judging them unfairly.

EXPRESSING THE JOY OF LIFE
"Brown, Beautiful and Talented."

It's no accident that this tribe produces a disproportionate number of expressive entertainers. People who contribute to the party and the group are important and highly valued. Creative and talented members of the Otara tribe have a high profile in mainstream New Zealand. Movies about the tribe's way of life break box office records and become an important source of social legitimacy. Being "brown, beautiful and talented" becomes a touchstone of the Otara tribe's place in wider society.

Humour is an important part of life in the Otara tribe—giving it richness and colour. "Humour is the one thing you can't take from us. It's our spirit". Humour unites and solidifies the group. It is a great leveller and position changer—you can poke fun at yourself, or the authorities or people who think they're better than you.

There is also the leavening effect of friends, family and community. This is a very sociable, gregarious tribe. Spending time together is by far the most enjoyable thing to do. Looking after your little brothers and sisters, seeing family members through tough times—that goes without saying—but feasting and laughing and dancing and singing—that's the joy of life.

The Lifestyle of the Otara Tribe

Work

The Otara tribe's work is typically either hard, boring or low-paid—often all of these. Typical jobs include factory processing work, industrial or domestic cleaning, truck or taxi driving, security work, construction or home care. A lot of petty controlling stuff goes on in their workplaces—bosses treating grown people like children. The Otara tribe love finding easier work with better conditions—not outdoors in cold weather, not lifting heavy loads or working in unsafe situations and not cleaning offices all through the night.

To many Otara tribe members, people are what turn a bad job into a tolerable or even enjoyable one. They don't have any great expectations that work will fulfil them or challenge them or make them rich, and they don't really want it to change their lives too much. Otara tribe members would rather adjust their expectations of what they're entitled to than move too far outside their work comfort zone. Working together in a gang, shearing, stonewalling or digging roadworks pay good money and let you have time with your mates. Working in a factory, a food outlet or in a call centre does the same for women.

Leisure

The Otara tribe's leisure is about family and friends. It's quite difficult for other tribes to really understand the extent of the bonding that happens between siblings or extended family members in this tribe. Family is who you are and what you do. You don't have to look outside for friends. The tribe's leisure activities are often very simple and spontaneous: parties, picnics, gathering food, visiting friends, and going to markets or shopping are all popular activities.

More elaborate feasts, weddings, hui and other functions provide an overall structure to tribe members' lives. Church is important for many people, and church-related activities are an important part of their social life. For young people, going out in a group with your family or friends to the movies, to housie or to the casino is common. Going out drinking isn't done by every tribe member, but among those who do it's often the main point of their leisure.

"Hanging with my mates, going for a walk, going to garage sales or giving the house a good spring clean" is a typical weekend for one female Otara tribe member. The men spend time on social sport, like touch rugby, softball or Pacific cricket if they're from the Islands.

Money

The sheer stress of lack of money is ever present in the Otara tribe. It can dominate lives, eroding relationships, starting rows that end in violence, and making it hard to think about the future. Most tribe members spend most of their money on the basic necessities of life. What's left — and sometimes even some of what's needed for the basics — goes to family or the church.

The Otara tribe's caring and sharing can cut to the bone. When you have just enough money for the electricity bill and your brother needs money to bail your nephew out of jail, sharing can require a strong belief that God will provide. The knowledge that, some day, you will be helped if you're in need isn't as much of a comfort as it will be when that time comes. Loan sharks and instant finance companies often fill the gap and preserve family harmony.

Gambling is common in this tribe. When money is short, a little bit can make a big difference — and it's nice to dream the big dream, even if you have no idea how you'd actually cope if you won. Having too much money is almost as bad for the Otara tribe as too little because it can move you outside your comfort zone.

Home

The Otara tribe's homes are typically rented and assets are few. Lower wages make it sensible for older children to stay at home and share their wages. It makes everything more predictable.

To the Otara tribe, home represents shelter, not style or status. It's where the basics of life are attended to. No one judges you by the value of your house. It's just where you live. However they may judge you by how clean it is. Keeping the place neat and tidy is a sign that you are managing well — coping is a high value in the Otara tribe.

Since members of this tribe tend not to own their own homes, there is more likely to be an emphasis on decoration with possessions rather than by changing the structure or the landscaping. The home may be filled with photographs, souvenirs from back home, things that the kids have made at school, and pretty ornaments. These things are not necessarily expensive, but vibrant and personal.

− 7 −
The Raglan Tribe

Found in:
Laid-back suburbs on the wild side of town, or small settlements in beautiful places.

Distinguishing Characteristics:
Old station wagons, stacks of firewood, mismatched possessions.

Whether they've been spat out of it, left it on their own terms, or just never got the point of it, Raglan tribe members don't belong to the mainstream. This tribe is far more contented when it feels it has flexibility and autonomy.

The key word for the Raglan tribe is freedom; its icons are the adventurer and the artist. Raglan tribe members want to create and control their own destiny. Their approach to authority is not so much defiance as indifference. They need to do what they need to do and if the rules don't fit then the rules are wrong.

The need to be free can express itself as a strong entrepreneurial spirit, and many of our most distinctive off-beat business success stories appear to have been driven by entrepreneurs with the Raglan spirit. These are the mavericks of New Zealand society — the people who did what the others only dreamed of.

The Raglan tribe seeks pleasure through experiences rather than things. Often members see accumulated possessions as a barrier or hindrance to doing what you want to do. They attach profound meaning to their experiences, whether they involve something creative or physically demanding or intensely emotional. In fact, they'll shy away from anything that doesn't hold their interest or whet their appetite for living. As workers, members of the Raglan tribe are better off without a boss. They're natural self-employed contractors, free-agent artisans and business owners.

The Signature Attitudes of the Raglan Tribe

MY LIFE, MY WAY

"I must create a system or be enslaved by another man's."

The Raglan tribe swims against the tide. These people are the annoying contrarians who zig when everyone else is zagging. Misfits. Their approach to authority is not so much defiance as indifference. They need to do what they need to do and if the rules don't fit then the rules are wrong. Tribe members often see themselves as the exception that proves the rule. Or the victim of bureaucracy gone mad.

The Raglan tribe comprises individuals who are often intensely internally driven. They're missing some of the genes of social embarrassment, and they have no real sense of a class structure or hierarchy or any other kind of social limit on who you can be. All they know is that when you feel yourself being driven by someone else's agenda, it's time to take control.

For the Raglan tribe, being in control of life is essential. Tribe members hate the idea of being trapped in another person's view of the world, whether that's a bleak 9-to-5 existence, a house in the suburbs with a picket fence, or a high-powered, buttoned-down desk job, putting up with idiots. They believe strongly that they know what's best for themselves — not so much "a man's house is his castle" as "don't fence me in!".

BEING WHO YOU ARE

*"Nothing I can do about it.
That's just the way I feel."*

Being true to yourself is not only a requirement of Raglan tribal membership, it's the justification for just about everything. Raglan tribe members prefer to respond intuitively rather than intellectually to events or people, and to be able to act naturally and genuinely—even if it's not the most appropriate way of operating. "Appropriate" isn't a word they use very much.

"Real" is though. Raglan tribe members can spot a fake a long way off. They prefer people who are unpretentious and open with real warmth or intensity—something to show they're alive and kicking. They're far more attuned to how people behave than what they say about themselves, though they'll accept you at face value till proven otherwise, and expect you to do the same.

As a result of this lack of pretence, there's often a kind of romantic excess to the Raglan tribe's view of the world—you see it in cultures as diverse as Celts, Maori and Italians. They dream and philosophise, explore and expand. Their minds are a bit more flexible than most so you often find this tribal mindset among people who are living alternative lifestyles and thinking alternative thoughts. Members of the Raglan tribe are likely to hold a range of quite contradictory or incongruous views that just happen to appeal to them.

EXPERIENCES, NOT POSSESSIONS
"I don't want to die wondering."

It's hard to explain to people who love shopping just how unimportant possessions are in the scheme of things. The Raglan tribe sees accumulated possessions as a barrier or hindrance to doing what you want to do. Unless they're actively enabling you to do or to be, the things you own are far more likely to slow you down or get in your way.

The Raglan tribe has a strong spiritual sense of themselves in the world. It attaches profound meaning to experiences, whether they involve something creative, or physically demanding, or intensely emotional. Gathering food becomes as much a conversation with the forces of the universe as does risking your life on the side of a mountain. Starting the business you always dreamed of is as much an expression of your inner being as is catching the perfect wave.

This tribe opens itself up to the joy of living—but also to the pain. It carries very little in the way of insulation. There will be scars. But there's also transcendence. And the ability to adapt yourself to new situations with the minimum of fuss. Raglan tribe members travel light.

IF IT DOESN'T FEEL RIGHT, DO SOMETHING ELSE

"If in doubt, don't."

There's an itinerant quality to the Raglan tribe that means even if they're quite settled in a place or a job or relationship, there's always the possibility they could pick up and leave at a moment's notice. More than most other tribes, they live on their wits and their emotions.

Their preference for going with the flow and following threads of interest and enjoyment means that these are not closed-off people. They know what they like and what endures. But their restlessness means they can be quite fickle, losing interest just as fast as it's captured.

People of many tribes harbour escape fantasies. The Raglan tribe puts them into practice—though few as dramatically as Barry Crump, who reputedly left a marriage by popping down to the shop for a paper and keeping on going.

When there's too much drama or too many obligations, Raglan has the capacity to just slide away. No big scenes, no fuss. Just suddenly not there anymore. Raglan tribe members are quite happy to fall off the administrative map, leaving no trace of where they've gone.

LIVING FOR TODAY

"I'll just keep doing it till I'm over it."

Remember when summer just seemed to go on and on as if it would never end. You were about eight. That's how it still is for the Raglan tribe. Time stands still. The present consumes them. Their past becomes a string of joined up peak experiences and their future offers more of the same.

There's no point getting ahead of yourself by thinking about the future. The Raglan tribe values spontaneity and the ability to respond fully to the moment. Raglan tribe members focus intensely on whatever they are doing, and in doing so they achieve "flow" — that timeless state where their physical effort or creativity or sense of pleasure simply overwhelm everything else.

For the Raglan tribe, this sense of engagement is coupled with a supreme confidence in their ability to respond to most eventualities. They are used to living on their wits, taking advantage of opportunities that arise, and doing what feels right at the time. It may take them to some crazy places but it means they're alive.

The Lifestyle of the Raglan Tribe

Work

There are typically two extremes to the Raglan tribe's working style. In the first, your work is seamlessly integrated into your life. The ultimate job is one where you get paid for doing what it is you love to do all day.

The Raglan spirit is also a profound motivation for

entrepreneurs. These are people who start their own businesses not because they dream of wealth and status, but because they value freedom and abhor having a boss. The business plan at the entrepreneurial end of the Raglan tribe is to start up and sell up as soon as the exit price will sustain the lifestyle they want to live.

At the other extreme, your work is whatever takes the least time out of your lifestyle. The aim is to work as little as possible or earn what you need in as few hours as possible. Many Raglan tribe members do whatever they can for three or four days a week so they can maximise their leisure on the other days. Shift work and contract work suit them. So does growing dope up in the hills somewhere. Or shifting with the seasons—ski jobs in winter, water jobs in summer.

Because their loyalty and commitment is low and their desire for flexibility and freedom is high, the Raglan tribe lives happily with the looser ties and uncertain future associated with contract work. These people are not worried about job security. It is a lifestyle far more sustainable for people who have talents or skills which are in short supply and earn better hourly rates.

Leisure

Leisure is the point of the Raglan tribal lifestyle. Your job title doesn't define you, your interests and pursuits do. Each tribal sub-group—hippies, surfers, musicians, artisans, adventurers—has a distinct aesthetic, language and dress style, immediately recognisable to each other.

Status comes from how good you are at the activities that define you and your tribe, not from your money. It's not about being seen in the right places, it's about being in the places no one else has ever seen. Making the first ascent or descent of a mountain or a river, exploring your inner spiritual depths in remote monastery, travelling through Africa in a house bus. These are the achievements that are considered heroic in the Raglan tribe and confer status on the achiever.

The Raglan tribe's activity is about peak pleasure, not about fame or fortune. Members don't boast about having been to a Rolling Stones concert; they rave about a kid they came across in a jungle town in Brazil playing Santana better than Carlos himself. The Raglan tribe's modus operandi is to travel light, land gently, experience fully and move on.

Money

Money comes and goes in this lifestyle. But don't ask Raglan tribe members where it goes. They don't care. They're missing the money gene. Many have no savings record to speak of and they doubt they'll ever get tied down to a big mortgage — better to pay cash and fix up an old bach by yourself or with a few mates, or build it yourself to your own design. Live off kai moana and swap a couple of hours work for some beer and potatoes. Or grow your own organic food at a fraction of the cost of the bought stuff.

The Kiwi make-do-and mend philosophy has a natural home in the Raglan tribe — Raglan tribe members won't waste money on things that don't matter. But the things that do matter to them will be "mint". Not flashy, but very good quality and well looked after.

In the Raglan tribe member's past there's almost always some kind of money and possession crisis that has caused them to shy away from a big spending lifestyle. Getting overstretched and having to sell something they loved; being cleaned out by burglars and realising how pointless it is to accumulate, lavishing a lot of cash on something flash only to have it pack up.

Home

The Raglan tribe member's home won't be a mess and it won't speak of money. But it will scream "laid-back-ness". These will be places that fit their distinctive lifestyle — whatever it is — a great deck for taking in the view, a big living room for spontaneous partying, a studio with lots of natural light.

There is a distinct tribal aesthetic. It's about things that are unusual and natural and personal. It's not about fashion or display. The Raglan tribe would never use imitation granite or veneer timbers when honest natural materials are available. Tribe members wouldn't buy new when there's old that will do the job as well or better.

It's about clever use of simple materials, perhaps in a new and interesting way to create comfortable living spaces that work for their users, fit well into their environment and make you feel uplifted in some way.

– 8 –
The Cuba Street Tribe

Found in:
Bohemian zones in central areas of main cities, at the coolest gigs, at art schools and universities.

Distinguishing Characteristics:
Looks weird, likes looking weird.

THE CUBA STREET TRIBE

The Cuba Street tribe is the avant-garde tribe — the cutting edge of society where trends are made and people live highly creative, rebellious lives. Members of the Cuba Street tribe are the weird ones whose shocking undertakings appal the mainstream, but also fascinate them, and more than likely are the harbingers of the next big shift in what's acceptable in society.

Cuba Street tribe members are the masters of the new. They're the culture makers, and in today's rapidly changing world, that gives this tribe an almost shaman-like aspect. Business, obsessed with "creativity" and "innovation", loves the creative originality of the Cuba Street tribe. They know that the trends come out of the Cuba Street tribe, and so they've embraced it into their heart. These people from the weird side are earning big money as designers, IT techno-wizards and marketing geniuses.

The Cuba Street tribe shares some signature attitudes with the Raglan tribe — most notably in relation to its rejection of the mainstream and the status they draw from their experiences. However, the Cuba Street tribe is unique in the energy it brings to defining itself, its focus on the new, and its thirst for experimentation. There's also the question of age. To get beyond 40 and remain a member of the Cuba Street tribe is a rare achievement. But that's prime territory for the Raglan Tribe.

The Signature Attitudes of the Cuba Street Tribe

MAINSTREAM SUCKS

"Let's get something straight — if this goes mainstream I'm out of here."

In the Cuba Street tribe, the biggest entry criteria is what you are not. Not straight, square, normal or average. This tribe despises any thought of conformity — damnation in the Cuba Street is a nice house in suburbs, a good job, chunky mortgage, lawnmowers on the weekend, 2.2 perfect children and a dog.

Cuba Street is the tribe with the will to be weird, and if the only behavioural prescription is that you aren't mainstream, it leaves a lot of space in which to express yourself. Anything that mocks or shocks the mainstream is cool. Non-conformity is respected across the board — skater, punk, hippy, stoner, muso, it's all cool, just so long as it's not normal.

There's a lot of room for self-expression in this attitude, but there are also a lot of pressures pulling Cuba Street tribe members back towards the middle of the road. For this reason, the Cuba Street tribe is the most transitory of the tribes. The Cuba Street tribe is full of twenty-somethings, but thins out as the ages rise, kids arrive and members head back to repeat their suburban upbringing with a tattoo as the souvenir of their time on the weird side.

ADDICTED TO THE NEW NEW THING

*"If I haven't seen something before,
it has a head start."*

The Cuba Street tribe lives in relentless pursuit of the next new thing — new music, new technology, new fashions, new drugs, new places, new ways of thinking. The tribal trend leaders will bring a steady stream of new ideas into the tribe. Some will be adopted widely, some won't.

The Cuba Street tribe's obsession is more with experiences than with things. Obsessing about possessing a new object purely for the sake of owning the object is not a Cuba Street tribe attitude. The "new new thing" is more likely to be a way of behaving, a new expression, a new place to hang out. If it is an object, then chances are it will be something that allows the owner to do something — a skateboard is a gateway to living the skater life, fashion statements like full-arm tattooing are an entry ticket for partying with the coolest crowd.

This isn't the same as the changing fashions that come to all the other tribes through the media. Those changes affect the Cuba Street tribe as well, but here, the transmission of the next new thing happens on the street. Cuba Street tribe members don't need to read Vogue magazine or Wired to know what's new; they see it in the flesh — some stylish cool chick in a bar, some DJ from Germany with weird new music.

The most viral of these new ideas spreads fast, out into the other tribes. Ironically, the newest new thing most often comes to the mainstream from the tribe that hates the mainstream most.

ANYTHING IS POSSIBLE

"Your future is one of limitless possibility."

In the Cuba Street tribe, there is no tall poppy syndrome hacking down those who stick their necks out. This is one reason why the tribe is the source of so many new trends in society.

The Cuba Street tribe is inhabited by optimists. Perhaps that comes from the preponderance of young people in the tribe, perhaps it's a function of the obsession with the new. Whatever the reason, in the Cuba Street tribe, there's no inbuilt sense of safety holding anyone back. It's full-throttle ahead, the bigger and more extreme the dream the better. Anything is possible.

This attitude removes the brakes on creativity that exist within many other tribes. As long as you're not selling out, there's no sense that any course of action is inevitable, no sense that any way of behaving is proscribed.

This attitude is a powerful motivator for new projects in the Cuba Street tribe. Most tribe members do have ambitious projects to match their big dreams for themselves. In the Cuba Street tribe, there's no answer to the question "why not?". Why shouldn't New Zealand music be treated with more respect than foreign music?

Why shouldn't you pursue unlikely goals or give substance to your mad imaginings?

BEING TRUE TO YOURSELF
"Life's about expressing your individuality."

In the Cuba Street tribe, the point of life isn't amassing stuff, it's expressing yourself through the way you live. This is a serious business. For all their outward live-for-the-day flippancy, many Cuba Street tribe members are driven by an inward-looking neurotic need to assert their uniqueness by continually reinventing themselves.

This act of living self-expressively is a serious and highly creative undertaking. Self expression can take many forms. The person might be consumed with a large, long-term creative project (perhaps an artistic project or a business) which becomes the larger expression of their identity. Or they might build up a unique identity from many small things, each an expression of personal preferences — a turn of phrase, unique dress style, a tattoo or the choice of which old car to drive.

Self expression is the creative flipside of the preoccupation with not being mainstream. Not being mainstream tells us what you are not; the urge for self expression defines who you are. And it's very hard work. While "mainstream" people are content to live in the suburbs with the outward signs of conformity all around them, Cuba Street tribe members don't take any detail of their lives for granted. Every aspect is considered as a potential vehicle for self expression.

REAL EXPERIENCE CREATES CRED

"The point of life is accumulating diverse new experiences."

The most potent status symbols of the Cuba Street tribe aren't the material trappings of the consumer society, but experiences on the edge. You get status for the stories you can tell, or better still, that others tell about you.

The most high-status experiences are the most avant garde — those closest to the cutting edge of culture. Hanging out with an alternative fashion diva. Playing with a rock legend. Skating with legendary skater. Getting away with the most audacious nose-thumbing at mainstream authority—spraying a sneaky stencil on a police car that comes to break up a party would do nicely.

Youth provides a great motivator for the accumulation of experiences. Many Cuba Street members feel their lack of life experience keenly and channel their energy into the headlong pursuit of their next new story.

The other reason Cuba Street tribe members collect experiences is to prove how different they really are. It's easy to talk the alternative talk and cultivate a look. But to create real cred you have to prove you've been to the weird side. The best way to do that is to get people telling stories about your escapades over there.

The Lifestyle of the Cuba Street Tribe

Work

There are two sorts of people in Cuba Street — those who are doing work they love and those who are doing work to support themselves doing what they love. The latter is much more common.

You find Cuba Street people at the cutting edge of arts and culture, technology and fashion. They're the ones doing the work for hardly anything at first — pulling the long hours, working their way up and paying their dues. Probably also thinking they're much better than other people who are getting paid lots more than them, but that's the necessary arrogance of Cuba Street.

The Cuba Street tribe is attracted to project work and short-term contracts — maybe with a steady underpinning of regular part-time work to keep the wolf from the door. But only just. There's an urgency to this tribe that forbids the accumulation of excess money just for its own sake.

Leisure

Leisure activities refuel the Cuba Street tank — even as they deplete the Cuba Street body. Partying ranges from a once-a-week-blow-out to a key element of daily life.

Leisure is mainly urban-based, highly social and highly lubricated with drugs and alcohol. It's often hard for these inner-city dwellers to escape the bright lights — and besides, many of them are refugees from the provinces, not anxious to return to the scene of former style crimes.

To the Cuba Street tribe, the countryside becomes a place you just have to pass through to get to wherever it is you really want to be — a beach, a ski field, or an alpine dance party. Road trips are exercises in balancing scarce finances with maximum fun and opportunities to grow legends.

Money

You never have enough money in the Cuba Street tribe, and sometimes it seems like you never will. The effects of compromising what you love for the sake of a few bucks are felt by almost every Cuba Street tribe member at some stage.

Feast and famine is the standard Cuba Street tribal style — mainly because the kind of work that might deliver a steady income is not the kind of work the Cuba Street tribe is attracted to. Increasingly though, the mainstream is embracing the creativity of the Cuba Street tribe and more of them are getting good jobs without having to sell out. The money gets spent on experiences — international travel, better drugs, more wicked clothes.

Home

There are two kinds of Cuba Street tribe homes — one is simply a place to exist; the other is a magnificent expression of the style and sensibilities of its occupants.

The eclectic nature of the tribe means that it's hard to characterise a particular environment as quintessentially Cuba Street, except that it won't necessarily have the standard items of status and conformity. You're extremely unlikely to see a La-Z-Boy recliner rocking chair unless its presence is a deeply ironic statement by the owner.

Probably the nearest you could come to a characterisation is that the houses are not trendy — yet. Cuba Street tribe homes are likely to contain a collection, or many collections, of objects once considered tacky — perhaps still considered tacky, but soon to be the new cool. Many of them are on the cutting edge of the next big trend; some will always be just plain weird. Some very cool Cuba Street homes were kitted out in mid-century modern retro in the 80s; it went mainstream in the 90s. Those same houses did 70s retro in the 90s; that's mainstreaming now. What's next for the mainstream? Get into Cuba Street homes to find out.

– 9 –

The Papatoetoe Tribe

Found in:

Suburbs and towns with concentrations of car-yards, supermarkets and sports grounds.

Distinguishing Characteristics:

Shift work, blue overalls, budgets.

The Papatoetoe tribe is the home of the Kiwi working man and woman whose approach to life is characterised by down-to-earth common sense, a focus on essentials, pride in physical achievement and a deep mistrust of intellectualism. Or as someone from Papatoetoe tribe might put it, "no frills, no wankers, get on with it and don't get up yourself".

Though this tribe is no longer as prevalent or as powerful as it once was, it has had a significant effect on the values and attitudes of many New Zealanders. Many Papatoetoe tribal attitudes have their origins in classic industrial-age, blue-collar values: hard work, solidarity with the workers and distrust of the bosses and educated types. That was the era of the state house, flagon of beer and an honest day's pay for an honest day's work.

In some key attitudes, the Papatoetoe tribe is closely related to the provincial heartland Balclutha tribe. The elements of shared character are particularly strong around egalitarianism, appreciation of hard work and the down-to-earth mistrust of intellectualism.

The reality of daily life in the Papatoetoe tribe might have moved on, but their priorities haven't changed much. Lifestyle in the Papatoetoe tribe is about the here and now. It's a place where the goals and dreams are down to earth: to keep a roof over your head, make enough money for a few extras, have a good life and see the kids do well. It's a simple plan — keep your head down, your nose clean, look after your own and make sure you get to enjoy yourself along the way.

The Signature Attitudes of the Papatoetoe Tribe

PHYSICAL RULES

"He's got everything: a gorgeous girlfriend and he can kick off both feet."

Glorification of the physical and derision of intellectualism are at the root of many attitudes in the Papatoetoe tribe. It's an attitude from the Papatoetoe tribe's industrial working-class past, and it survives into the post-industrial world, where you're just as likely to find members of the Papatoetoe tribe doing white-collar clerical jobs as on the factory floor.

The primacy of the physical starts with how you look. This is especially true for women, and in these metrosexual times, it's even true for men. The good-looking pecking order exists in every tribe, but in the Papatoetoe tribe it's more fundamental because there are few other pecking orders to compete with it. For a girl of the Papatoetoe tribe, being pretty could mean you really didn't need to strive to develop other attributes or skills.

The one source of status that does compete with good looks — and overrides it completely in men — is sporting prowess. The sports field is at the apex of the Papatoetoe tribal cult of the physical — the more physical or dangerous the game, the greater status you acquire. The big hits of rugby league top the list, with other forms of rugby and motor sports close behind. More cerebral games such as cricket, with its love of elegant strokes and its spindly limbed players, are treated with suspicion at best. In cricket, it took our greatest uncoached natural, freezing-worker Lance Cairns, with his brute-strength-and-natural-eye batting style to create our first true working-class cricket hero.

In sports, the greatest status goes to the uncoached natural — free from the suspicion of intellectualism, and if possible, aided by natural strength and power.

HANDS ARE SMARTER THAN BOOKS
"You don't learn common sense out of a book."

Practical skills are highly valued by the Papatoetoe tribe—the ability to do things with your hands is an honest virtue. What you might call constructive intelligence is highly prized. To be described as "clever" in a Papatoetoe tribal setting generally means you've got a great skill with your hands in some way. "A clever chippie" can get you through the trickiest building dilemmas, but don't bother testing him with the cryptic crossword.

"Clever" really describes common sense, and the Papatoetoe tribe places great store in it. Common sense is the great honest virtue—being practical, but not so smart you're putting yourself above your mates. This tribe believes that most academic achievers are hopelessly impractical twits with no sense—common or otherwise. They might do OK in book work, but try them on building something or stripping a motor.

Hard work goes hand in hand with common sense. Evidence of hard work is a sign of a good bloke or a capable woman. Few will know what life's like with the cushion of extra money, so the practical skills of keeping life under control are very important, whether we're talking about budgeting, DIY or traditional home-making skills like sewing and baking.

When people from the Papatoetoe tribe do home improvements, they do them themselves. When they get creative, they express themselves through making practical objects for the garage, garden or house. To the Papatoetoe tribe, there are few satisfactions as great as the cold beer in the sun on the deck you just finished building.

DON'T GET UP YOURSELF

"We're all equal so don't go around thinking you're better than me."

The tall-poppy syndrome may well have originated in the Papatoetoe tribe and it is still flourishing there. The cardinal rule is: don't stand out too far and don't go around acting like you're better than everyone else.

This is the great Kiwi egalitarian tradition. It's the tradition of the boss who rolls his sleeves up and gets stuck in with the workers, the neighbours who lend a hand pouring concrete, the friends who do the dishes when they come over for tea. For those who play by the rules, it's an inclusive, accepting world. You can even stand out from the crowd if you don't get up yourself.

The Mad Butcher is a magnificent example of a Papatoetoe tribe tall poppy — he stands out but is loved for it because he matches each of his outlandish acts with a self-deprecating celebration of a Kiwi battler he knows. The Butcher's support for Papatoetoe's great sporting icon, The Warriors, feeds his credibility. The worse the Warriors do, the more cred the Butcher gets for his unwavering loyalty to the battling underdogs.

The only place where tall poppies are regularly celebrated and encouraged by the Papatoetoe tribe is on the sports field — but only if you're very good and very unconcerned about how good you are. In fact, exaggerated humility in the face of great achievement is possibly the greatest Papatoetoe tribal virtue of all. The brilliant scorer of the match winning try must always divert any praise and credit the team.

But off the sports field, you don't want to be seen as a try-hard — especially if you're doing something academic. In high school, a pass mark is by far the best result. To strive to excel at something intellectual is viewed with suspicion by your peers, a sign you've started thinking you're better than your mates. Thinking like that will get you exiled from this tribe fast.

LIFE'S NOT FAIR, SO JUST GET ON WITH IT

"No one else is going to do it for you. Head down, bum up, get on with it."

In the Papatoetoe tribe, lives are often lived with very little margin for error. Rushing between jobs, juggling kids and work hours, making this month's payments. It doesn't stop for anything. So when things go wrong there's no room for dwelling on what might have been. Head down and bum up — that's the correct response.

Externally, there's little sympathy for people who are the authors of their own misfortune — "should've thought of that, shouldn't you?", "You've made your bed, now lie in it." But just quietly there's recognition that "that could have been me if I'd made a few different decisions".

Although preoccupied with getting on with it, the Papatoetoe tribe does its share of complaining and has a lot of resentment towards those in charge—especially if they throw their weight around. There's a sense of the indignant victim in this mindset—they work hard but see other people get the profits and the fat salaries.

There's a flipside to getting on with it—getting away with it. The Papatoetoe tribe lives with a profound sense of inevitability, it doesn't believe it can change the system; there's no grand overthrow strategy. But minor skirmishes are constantly undertaken around the edges of the battlefield. Evening up the ledger—whether it's taking home some office supplies or a little of the company's finished product—is seen as a legitimate perk, not theft. You can't beat the system, but if you can get away with something, have a go.

A BETTER VERSION OF THE SAME LIFE

"Get comfortable and cruise."

Few members of the Papatoetoe tribe seriously aspire to a significantly different life from the one they grew up in. Most often the aspiration is for a better version of that life—a nicer house, a better boat, longer holidays. The concept of reinventing yourself is not one this tribe is comfortable with. Start thinking like that, that you could be better than the mates you grew up with, and you'll be thrown out for the North Shore or Grey Lynn tribes to squabble over.

For many in the Papatoetoe tribe, life isn't something that unfolds according to a master plan. Instead it tends be a journey from one intermediate goal to another — a new TV, the wedding, a holiday, a new car. The overall shape of life isn't something to be planned to a great extent. Your life is just something that happens along the way. "You work hard. You get by. You have a laugh. Then you wake up one morning and look back and say, Jesus, I've done quite a bit haven't I?"

Of course, the Papatoetoe tribe still dreams big. It's just that dreams and aspiration are often tempered by the tribe's signature realism — "life's tough, dreaming's fine but it doesn't pay the bills". This tribe is grounded in the hard reality of the here and now.

Most big dreams that do manage to survive tend to hinge on an extraordinary stroke of luck. The dream of the big win — on Lotto, the TAB or at the Casino. Or the dream of the small win — the pokies at the pub are prime Papatoetoe territory.

The Lifestyle of the Papatoetoe Tribe

Work

In the Papatoetoe tribe, work is what you do to pay the bills, it's not about personal fulfilment or advancement. The dream is to score a well-paying job that requires the least work and has the best perks — you're making money and you're beating the system.

The nuclear family is at the heart of the Papatoetoe tribe's work ethic. Jobs are what you do to provide for your family; many couples work different shifts so that one parent is always there for the kids.

Work itself is often resented in much the same way school was; it's an overbearing authority which takes up your time and stops you doing what you'd really like to. But those long shifts — well at least you get some decent time off — time for shopping (her) or working on the car (him), or spending time with the kids (them).

Men from the Papatoetoe tribe often do manual work — as tradesmen, labourers, or shift workers in factories. More than likely it will be physically demanding in one way or another. Women of the Papatoetoe tribe tend to be in administrative or service positions — retail sales, call-centre work, merchandising. Maybe helping others look good — working as a hairdresser, beautician or gym instructor. Working part time while they bring up their kids.

Leisure

In the Papatoetoe tribe, life is what happens in the time after work. That's about family and friends and having fun together. Hanging out with your mates is at the heart of the Papatoetoe tribe's social life. Social circles are long-standing and important sources of fun and entertainment. Many friendships will go back to childhood. Often members are still living in the areas they were born into.

For men from the Papatoetoe tribe, their cars, their mates, their sport and their kids tend to rule their leisure activities. Time pressures mean their leisure is often based on an activity rather than just kicking back with a few beers in front of the TV. They like to muck about fixing things and building stuff together. Or fishing.

For women, leisure is about talking, drinking, shopping for clothes, exercise, and hobbies. A night out with the girls is a regular part of the social calendar. But once you have kids it's hard to find time for yourselves. "My husband and I went out on a date together and as we were driving down the motorway he said to me "let's go back and get the kids". And I said "No we can do this."

Money

The Papatoetoe tribe's attitudes to money reveal two distinct sub-groups. The first is the Credit Junkie — based on the availability of easy credit and deferred payments. The second is the traditional thrifty Kiwi battler, whose goal is to pay his or her way without owing anyone anything.

Credit Junkies want to enjoy life today because the future may never come. They buy new on hire purchase — no payments until 2008. They take all the credit they can get and have the life they want now, even if that means paying for it in a hazy distant future.

In contrast, the Thrifty hates debt. The philosophy is simple: no frills until you can afford them and don't get out of your depth. These people clip coupons, join Christmas clubs, save through banks or credit unions, and thrive on finding bargains. They'll get something second-hand on Trade Me rather than splash out. Thrifties take great pride in the fact that they are not dependent on the state, and they'll save systematically. There'll be a budget that they stick to and a plan. But they won't be doing it to fulfil some grand dream; this strategy is about achieving a better version of the same life — not getting above yourself.

Home

Home ownership is what distinguishes the Papatoetoe tribe from its poorer cousins. It may not be very grand, and it's certainly not in the best street. In big cities it may not even be in a particularly safe and secure area, but it's a major achievement. A testament to years of support from your family and going without luxuries.

There may not be a well developed garden — there's no time for that. But the lawn will be tidy and if there are kids, there'll be a trampoline or a swing set in the back yard. There will almost certainly be a garage. And in it will be a pretty nice car. Maybe two. Ford or Holden. Not both.

It's not unusual to find adult children living at home in the Papatoetoe tribe—often with a boyfriend or girlfriend in tow. They probably did go flatting for a while but it's tough to make ends meet on a low-wage job or an apprenticeship. It's comfortable at home and you can save for what you really want.

– 10 –
Your Tribal Profile

So what tribe are you? Some people immediately feel like they belong to one tribe. Others recognise more than one tribe in themselves. The 8 Tribes aren't exclusive sets, they're groups with fluid boundaries. Many of us straddle more than one tribe.

Imagine that everyone in New Zealand was gathered together in a huge crowd. Then we shuffled them about until every person had the people whose attitudes were most similar to theirs, standing next to them.

The result would be a series of overlapping circles. Eight circles. Some large, some small. In the centre of each circle, attitudes would be very similar. The people standing there would have a lot of attitudes in common and they would clearly identify themselves as belonging only to one tribe. If you already have a very clear idea which tribe you belong to, you're probably close to the centre of that group.

However, as we head towards the edge of each circle, we find more diverse attitudes, more overlap and cross-over between the tribes. If you think you straddle more than one tribe, you're probably in one of these positions.

Many of us draw our tribal identity from more than one source. If you grew up in one setting and ended up somewhere very different, you probably retain some of the marker attitudes of the earlier tribe. If you have to live one sort of life but would rather be living another, that will reflect itself in your signature attitudes. Living with someone from another tribe almost always means you get a bit of tribal cross-over happening. Or a lot of fights.

The easy way to check is to go to our 8 Tribes website www.8tribes.co.nz and complete the free tribal profile.

– 11 –

8 Trends

We've called the 8 Tribes the hidden classes of contemporary New Zealand, but that doesn't mean that they're set in stone.

The tribes system is changing all the time; attitudes evolve, relationships between the different tribes alter. There's no universally accepted tribal pecking order and there are many power dynamics at work in the tribal interrelationships.

The shifting economic, political and cultural fortunes of each tribe drives the sometimes subtle, sometimes overt exercise of influence by one tribe over the others. Many of the significant social trends in New Zealand can be explained in terms of this inter-tribal balance of power. In this section we examine the tribal interplay behind eight trends that are having a profound impact on New Zealand society right now.

TREND ONE: THE DEFINING TENSION

The educated influencers of the North Shore and Grey Lynn tribes are locked in a battle for influence.

The defining tension of our times is the battle for influence between the Grey Lynn and North Shore tribes. Both are big meritocratic tribes; they're the tribes of education, achievement and influence. They're also the tribes that run the country day-to-day. They make up the majority of our professionals, managers, policy makers, regulators, commentators and influencers.

They agree on many things, such as the value of education, the power of technology, the need for progress. But within these broad frames of agreement there are some fundamental differences. For the North Shore tribe, education is a means of advancement for individuals, a ticket to a better job and a richer nation. For the Grey Lynn tribe, education is a passport to cultural and intellectual riches, but also a device for the empowerment of the less fortunate and the creation of a more just society.

This basic tension between the Grey Lynn tribe's belief in the collective good and North Shore tribe's belief in the advancement of individuals is at the root of many of the battles for influence that we see between these tribes.

Nowhere is this tension expressed more completely than in the on-going battle between bureaucrats and business. The Grey Lynn tribe has gained ascendancy in Government. Parliament and the public service (with the likely exception of the Treasury) are both dominated by the Grey Lynn tribe. The world of business is clearly North Shore tribe territory.

Occasionally the North Shore-Grey Lynn tribal battle gets public and nasty. The Resource Management Act has provided many memorable battles, with forces massing behind the North Shore tribe's banners of profit, progress and individual rights, and the Grey Lynn tribe's principled stand on preserving the environment. The recent spat over the Whangamata marina resource consent was a classic case of this in action — the Minister of Conservation championed the Grey Lynn tribe's principles of preservation, only to have his ban on progress overturned in court in a great North Shore tribe victory. As they say in the North Shore tribe, "he who knows the rules best, wins".

Of course it's not all defeats for the Grey Lynn tribe. It's knocked back more than a few car races, motorway proposals and harbour side developments in the recent past. Long term, the trend is for Grey Lynn tribal principles to enter North Shore tribal thinking. Ideas that start out radical become gradually become mainstream. The greening of business, widespread adoption of recycling, social innovations such as civil unions and consumer rights legislation, all show this trend in action.

TREND TWO: PONSONBY IS THE NEW REMUERA

A new elite tribe emerges of conspicuous consuming, highly discerning influencers.

The New Zealand power elite used to operate strictly according to Remuera tribal rules. Influence was something for white folks with well rounded vowels, a private school education, plenty of old money and a good Remuera tribe family pedigree.

Now the currency of influence has changed. The old Remuera tribe power elite has been gently displaced by a new group that combine the North Shore tribe's urge to achieve and acquire, the Grey Lynn tribe's love of sophistication and culture, and a touch of the iconoclastic spirit of the Cuba Street tribe. We call it the Ponsonby proto-tribe.

Ponsonby proto-tribe members are the new influencers, the most successful children of the knowledge economy. The currency that gets you admission to this rarefied group is a track record of achievement, intelligence and worldly sophistication.

The Ponsonby proto-tribe is made up of highly educated, cosmopolitan global citizens. They're the self-made leading lights of the knowledge society who are the all-productive "makers". Some are money makers—clever dealmakers, visionary entrepreneurs and brand builders. Others are culture makers, who wield their influence through their ability to capture the imagination—the film makers, artists and celebrities. They're often deeply principled, spiritual seekers who, having attained material wealth, may lose interest in acquiring more money and turn their minds to the important business of living well.

What they all share is a track record of having changed the world in some way. If they're a money maker, they haven't just made money, they've also built brands that millions love, or companies that have shaped our society. If they are culture makers, they're not admitted to the Ponsonby proto-tribe just for being famous; they're rated because their contribution to our culture, as a film maker or artist or actor, has been significant.

A generation ago, the wealthy influencers of the Remuera tribe slipped easily into anonymous philanthropy as they attained a certain stature. When their Ponsonby proto-tribe counterparts of today want to give something back, they look for how they can change the world. Wellington infrastructure investor Lloyd Morrison is a classic case. His gift to our society is a campaign to change the flag to a black silver fern.

The Ponsonby proto-tribe hasn't completely abandoned the Remuera model of refined elitism. They are hedonistic consumers who live very well and don't feel guilty about it, but they shrink from the obvious status symbols of the North Shore tribe. There are no jet skis or flash baches in Pauanui for the people of the Ponsonby proto-tribe. Instead they practice intellectual materialism—that beautiful and discerning half-caste child of the North Shore and Grey Lynn tribes' uneasy union. The value of an object is a combination of its scarcity, its monetary value and its intellectual qualities.

Their weekend boltholes are in pristine natural environments, accessible only from the water. Their clothes and accessories are designer, but obscure designers that most people wouldn't know. They're comfortable mixing designer with cheap and fun; they're big on vintage.

They believe in a better world. They are environmentalists and social liberals. They care, and they take action, trying to live a more eco-friendly lifestyle and lending their names and money to support campaigns to right wrongs. Think "walking lightly on the earth in designer shoes".

TREND THREE: GLORIFICATION OF THE NEW

The Cuba Street tribe goes from weird to wanted.

Never before has the "new new thing" had so much value as it does in today's modern capitalist world. Product cycles and fashion trends come and go faster than ever. The buzziest buzz words of business are innovation, ideas, creativity. Market analysts look for new directions, new revenue streams, entire new markets. The formerly stodgy scholars of academia are all hungry to invent their own hot new theory. The media constantly hunts the holy grail of the newest new thing, gives it five minutes of fame and suddenly it's old news, last week's thing. So what's next?

It's a world made for Cuba Street tribe. Once they were the freaky rebels and fringe dwellers that respectable people shied away from. Now their weirdness is the hottest commodity in business and the media. Everyone wants the new new thing, and nobody understands it better than non-conformists of the Cuba Street tribe.

It used to be that you'd straighten up your act to get a job in the corporate world, get a hair cut, lose the nose ring, buy some straight clothes. Not any more, at least not at the creative end of business. These days more and more brands want to be "edgy", they want to have the next new look before their competitors do — ads with the latest soundtrack or the cutting edge animation style that makes them first. Cuba Street tribe members are welcomed into the plum creative jobs, as designers, programmers, video editors and copy writers. Their managers from the North Shore and Grey Lynn tribes love the weirdness — "oh yes, plenty of tattoos and piercings here, we're a creative business."

One effect of this phenomenon has been the mainstreaming of weirdness. Looking different used to carry a social stigma, these days it's a valid fashion statement to look like you live on the non-conformist fringe. As a result, Cuba Street tribal fashions make rapid entry into the mainstream as members of the North Shore and Grey Lynn tribes attempt to declare their creative, non-conformist credentials. The body piercings and tattoos that signal credibility to mainstream tribes seeking edginess are now about as alternative and cutting edge as wearing Levis.

TREND FOUR: WOW, WE'RE FUNKY AND BROWN

The Otara tribe fertilises the Cuba Street tribe and New Zealand falls in love with home-grown pop culture.

Remember when people wanted a quota for Kiwi music played on the radio? Remember in the 80s when "New Zealand music" meant a slightly discordant guitar-band of pasty white boys from the Cuba Street tribe? Back then, New Zealand music was a non-conformist punk-inspired Cuba Street tribal fashion statement—"I'm not mainstream, I listen to New Zealand music". The other tribes cringed and Kiwi popular culture was overwhelmingly imported.

Things have changed. Kiwi popular culture has been infiltrated by New Zealanders. No matter what our tribe, we're listening to Kiwi music, watching Kiwi films, reading Kiwi words, wearing Kiwi fashion.

This cultural revolution began when the browning of New Zealand added new dimensions to the creative fringe. The Otara and Cuba Street tribes cross-fertilised to produce a new, brown urban New Zealand street culture that New Zealanders from every urban tribe have fallen in love with.

You see it in the new distinctive genre of Aotearoa hip hop and roots music. Bands like Fat Freddy's Drop and performers like Che Fu and Scribe are who we listen to by choice. It's in the explosion of Polynesian-inspired street fashion being worn by every tribe—pounamu pendants and tattoos reflecting traditional Maori and Polynesian patterns. It's in the indigenous movies, like Sione's Wedding and Whale Rider, that have broken box office records over the past few years. It's in the singing of the Maori version of the national anthem at rugby games, something that began as a shocking act of defiance when Hinewehi Mohi dared to sing only E ihoa at Twickenham in 1999, but has now slipped easily into the rugby pre-test tradition.

The result is a nation far more comfortable in its skin. Conservative Kiwis are choosing Kiwi cultural products ahead of the foreign competitors. The new All Black haka receives a special cheer because we know what it signifies. The cultural cringe of previous generations is being replaced by a boisterous pride in these unique cultural expressions. "Listen to our music," we're telling our foreign friends. The shape of our islands has suddenly become a fashion statement to be worn on tee-shirts and added to CD covers. It seems the quota won't be necessary after all.

TREND FIVE: ETHICAL CONSUMPTION

The Grey Lynn tribe teaches the world to do business with principles.

Consumerism has never meshed well with Grey Lynn tribe principles. Grey Lynn tribe members have never believed that profit and growth are an end in themselves; they want business to be good for society and good for the environment.

After more than a decade of consumer activism that exposed global consumer brands using child labour and revolted against the worst polluters of the environment, the Grey Lynn tribe's principles are shaping a whole new branch of ethical, guiltless consumption. It seems it may be possible for the thinking, caring consumers of Grey Lynn to have their cake and eat it too.

One of the keys to this development is "off-setting", a new process of compensating for the social and environmental effects of being a 21st century human. You offset the carbon emissions your lifestyle creates by planting trees. You calculate the food miles of your meals — how far it travelled to get to your plate — so that you're eating food that's both fresher and less environmentally damaging. You neutralise the effect of your presence on the earth and you want the firms you deal with to do the same.

The Grey Lynn tribe's growing economic power as discerning customers, investors, communicators and, importantly, as the brains behind many successful international businesses, means they've gained serious business credibility in the 21st century. Google's motto "Don't Be Evil" illustrates a hip new attitude to growth and wellbeing. Bill Gates legitimises Microsoft's dominant market position by investing billions to fight malaria, AIDS and world poverty.

Film documentaries coming out of the US — like An Inconvenient Truth; Enron: The Smartest Guys in the Room; and Michael Moore's classic, Roger and Me — point to the anti-social effects of unconstrained corporate greed. Books like Naomi Klein's No Logo and Eric Schlosser's Fast Food Nation become best sellers.

The Grey Lynn tribe has long admired The Warehouse founder Stephen Tindall, because he created a lot of jobs and pursued philanthropic goals alongside his business goals. Now, when the Grey Lynn tribe is asked to name admirable New Zealand businesses, they mention firms they regard as cool eco-businesses — Whale Watch, Untouched World, MacPac and Icebreaker.

The Grey Lynn tribe's growing influence has seen the spread of this thinking from the intellectual edges of society into the mainstream. The North Shore tribe is embracing these ethical business ideas, and they're becoming embedded within the mainstream business world. Organisations such as the New Zealand Business Council for Sustainable Development are gaining credibility and influence. North Shore tribe accountants and consultants have seized the opportunity and are specialising in multiple bottom-line reporting. Even industrial companies are getting with it. It's a measure of the Grey Lynn tribe's influence that New Zealand's largest electricity generator, Meridian Energy, can view a green energy-only approach as a valid business strategy.

TREND SIX: THE RETURN OF THE GOLDEN WEATHER

The Raglan Dream becomes a cultural legend.

Every tribe has its counterpart in other countries, but the Raglan tribe is perhaps more characteristic of New Zealand than of anywhere else. This may be why its significance to many mainstream urban Kiwis from the North Shore and Grey Lynn tribes is growing. The Raglan tribal ideal — the Raglan Dream — the chilled-out coastal life, living close to nature without the material trappings of the modern world, has become enshrined in the national cultural memory as a quintessential expression of Kiwiness.

The universal symbol of the Raglan ideal — the Kiwi bach — is assuming mythic proportions. Like the kakapo, it has become a threatened species, and its passing is often lamented. Many commentators would have us believe that every Pakeha family once had a family bach at a beach that was its turangawaewae. The family returned every year to this heart-place and learned to live to the simple rhythms of nature, in peaceful harmony.

The advertising industry loves this myth. Sweeping shots of coastline, golden sand beaches, tanned sandy-haired kids and their little Maori mates populate this world of innocent egalitarian adventure around the fibrolite shack. It's an image that's been used to sell everything from financial services to health insurance and phone calls.

The power of the Raglan Dream is intensifying as it becomes increasingly distant from the truth. The Government launches rescue packages to save the traditional Kiwi campground. Workaholic commuters of the North Shore and Grey Lynn tribes seek refuge in the dream of perpetual summer in a basic bach. They buy coastal land in increasing numbers. Beautiful, sparsely populated areas like Golden Bay and the Coromandel get more and more absentee owners and property values rocket. The edges of cliffs and shores and the slopes and tops of hills with views sprout new building sites. Baby boomers invest their retirement savings in a view.

For the majority who can't afford to buy this full-blown Raglan Dream, there is still a way out of the rat race — adopt the growing city lifestyle we call Urban Raglan.

Urban Raglan is the lifestyle being lived by increasing numbers of city-dwellers, mostly from that caste of professionals who are good at what they do, make good money, but just can't bring themselves to take it all seriously.

Urban Raglan is about living a pared down, stripped back existence where balance and well-being trump ambition and achievement. These people go to work alongside their North Shore and Grey Lynn tribe neighbours, but don't buy into their respective status games. Their lives are peppered with small symbols of rebellion — the old car, the offbeat office dress sense, the surfboard in the car ready for a cruise past the beach on the way home — life's about always being ready for when the wind turns offshore.

TREND SEVEN: WINNING IS EVERYTHING

The North Shore religion of competition and winning has spread from sports to entertainment, reinforcing the message that life is a contest — on every level.

The North Shore tribe's obsession with winning, competing and measuring achievement is spreading through the other tribes. Ranking just about everything from winner to loser is our preoccupation. No matter what it is, there's a constantly polling-rolling-totalled league table to measure it on winner-loser scale — the world-ranking of our internet speeds, the decile ratings of our children's schools, our economic growth rate, our sports teams' rankings, the popularity ratings of the media, the most eligible bachelor, health rankings...

We measure the worth of prominent people on the winner-loser scales such as the rich list, CEO salary list, the writer who sells the most books, the artist who fetches the most at auction, the New Zealander most recognised in America. We measure ourselves by the OECD ratings and magazine polls of the coolest travel destination.

We worship our winners. The media loves nothing more than a "Kiwi world-beater". Our world-beating sports heroes are afforded remarkable attention, particularly if they play an Olympic sport. The government sports agency SPARC sets medal targets for each sport and cuts their funding if they fall too far below them. Why? So we can register a number in the gold column of the Olympic Games medal table — and become the greatest performing Olympic nation — per capita.

It's an obsession that's come from the highly competitive

battle raging daily in the North Shore tribe, and it has influenced all the others. Even the Grey Lynn tribe have caught the winning fever. After a brief flirtation with "participation is the point" in the mid 90s, they're back bemoaning our atrocious ranking on all manner of global tables—we should be ashamed of our pitiful world ranking on the tables for child abuse, deforestation, carbon emissions, water pollution, overseas aid and refugee settlement.

Perhaps the greatest sign that we're obsessed with winning throughout society is the transformation of light entertainment into gladiatorial blood sport via reality TV. Once we spent primetime watching light entertainment shows with singing and dancing. Now we watch celebrities and ordinary people battle it out against each other for the right to be crowned the champion of tropical beach games, ballroom dancing or home renovation.

TREND EIGHT: REGAINING OUR VIRGINITY

The Grey Lynn tribes hanker after paradise lost with religious fervour.

On Raoul Island, New Zealand's isolated territorial outpost, there's a weeding programme to remove the exotic plant species that have found their way, literally, to the middle of nowhere. This pristine environment, more than 1000 kilometres from either New Zealand or Tonga, isn't designed to be seen. Just to be pure — and there.

On the mainland islands of New Zealand we are constantly shown the predations on the natural environment of stoats, ferrets, rats, deer, goats, dairy cows, wild horses, possums, dogs, cats and of course, humans themselves. Simply by living, it seems, we destroy paradise.

The Grey Lynn tribe feels this acutely and has set out to save us from ourselves. Now, Grey Lynn tribe members not only want to know that somewhere far away there are pristine, unpolluted, predator-free environments supporting life in some primeval form, they want them close to urban areas. With the support of the Raglan tribe, Grey Lynn tribe agitators and bureaucratic insiders champion marine reserves, mainland islands, replanting native flora, new green spaces and the eradication of exotic species. They preach the doctrine of biodiversity, resonant with moral principles, higher learning and the sanctity of ancient life.

At times it seems that the doctrine of conservation and native regeneration is a war waged with a near religious fervour. It's little wonder; the Grey Lynn tribe has created an ideology to fuel the fight that descends directly from 19th century ideas about the noble savage and the evangelical Christian tradition.

According to this thinking, the world was once an unspoilt Garden of Eden inhabited by technologically primitive but morally wise people. With technology and progress came moral corruption and environmental ruination. But now that we have evolved, we are ready to recreate that virgin paradise of an untouched planet. We're going to reinvent ourselves with the wisdom of those noble savages, minus the slash-and-burn cultivation and cannibalism. We will reverse the collateral damage of human predation—saving helpless victims like kakapo and whales, expelling from the Garden of Eden the exotic plants and intruder animals that feast on virtuous native flora and fauna. Through this process we'll reinvent earthly paradise as it was before original sin.

The intellectual ancestors of today's environmental crusaders were motivated by the promise of ascending into heaven to hear the choirs of angels. Nothing's really changed — our latter-day crusaders' heaven-on-earth is a fully regenerated native forest, and their angels the fully restored dawn chorus.

All this suggests that the Grey Lynn tribe's environmental crusade to preserve and regenerate primeval New Zealand is more than a passing fad, and there will be fertile ground for this message among the other tribes too. It also suggests that when the conservation lobby picks a battle, expect them to have the moral fortitude for a very long fight.

− 12 −
8 Tribes and the Future

So what is the future for each of the 8 Tribes? In the ebb and flow of the evolving 8 Tribes system, some tribes appear to have a flourishing future, others are headed for more uncertain times.

In the flourishing corner, the North Shore, Grey Lynn, Raglan, Cuba Street and Otara tribes will continue to grow in influence.

The North Shore tribe will continue to increase in size, drawing its energy from the accelerating momentum of consumer society and the enduring urge to acquire the next new thing. The Grey Lynn tribe will grow with the knowledge industries and the post-materialist urge to attend to every detail of life as if it were an issue of planetary survival.

8 TRIBES AND THE FUTURE

The Cuba Street tribe will boom because it feeds the consumer beast with a steady stream of cultural novelty and enlivens jaded intellects with outrageous new propositions. The Otara tribe will grow in cultural influence through the efforts of its talented children, from the production line Pacific Islands All Black heroes to the fresh cultural phenomena of Pacific hip hop, Maori Television and bro'Town.

The Raglan tribe will grow because it's selling the rat race the dream of living where the living is easy. In our affluent society, where working as a free agent is an increasingly viable option, expect more and more people to opt for freedom and take the path of the Raglan tribe.

We can't help feeling that the Balclutha tribe is at the high tide of its influence over the other tribes. Its white heartland culture is being usurped by a browner, more urban expression — less "gidday mate", more "chur bro".

The future looks even bleaker for the Remuera and Papatoetoe tribes. The Remuera tribe's demise will continue as the shadow of our colonial past fades. This tribe seems doomed to go the way of the private schools that were once its cornerstone institutions, now annexed by the North Shore tribe and converted from places that schooled the subtle arts of Remuera tribe elitism, into bootcamps that teach the North Shore science of winning.

The Papatoetoe tribe too seems to be out of step with the times. There are huge pressures on this tribe to join the North Shore tribe's status elevator; those that don't will increasingly be consigned to the economic underclass—a very unattractive selling proposition.

Perhaps the biggest shift in prospect for the 8 Tribes system is the emergence of a whole new tribe, the Ponsonby tribe of cultural producers and peddlers of economic influence.

Right now Ponsonby is a proto-tribe—a growing cluster of influential networks and crystallising patterns of behaviour, but not yet with its own distinctive set of signature attitudes. We predict that these networks will harden into a full-blown new tribe. How long will that take? It could take a surprisingly short time. Cultural transmission happens fast these days.

8 TRIBES AND THE FUTURE

At the start of this study we explained our frustration with the widespread acceptance of the idea of the typical New Zealander—the hard-working, friendly, down-to-earth, can-do Kiwi. Having completed this project, it's clear to us that this view of our national character probably does describe the few common qualities we share as New Zealanders.

But that's not where you find our compelling stories. The things we share are the least interesting things about us. In science as in life, opposites attract. It's tension, pressure, friction and collisions that create energy. It's the same with our culture. What is remarkable about New Zealanders, and what creates the energy within our society is not our sameness; it's the differences between us all.

As the widespread pan-tribal popularity of the street culture that has flowered from the Otara—Cuba Street tribe cross-pollination shows, the more we celebrate our differences and let them rub up against each other, the more vitality and vibrance we create, and the more we like ourselves.

Our contention is that this interaction between the tribes is where the most compelling expressions of the national character of New Zealand are to be found. It's in the interplay between different tribal attitudes going on every day in our homes, our workplaces, our schools, our pubs, on buses and on our sports fields.

There is no typical New Zealander. What is distinctive about us is the sum total of our differences. It's the friction, the antagonism, the understanding and the celebration that goes on between all the 8 Tribes all the time that defines us as New Zealanders.

At the start of this study we explained our frustration with the widespread acceptance of the idea of the typical New Zealander—the hard-working, friendly, down-to-earth, can-do Kiwi. Having completed this project, it's clear to us that this view of our national character probably does describe the few common qualities we share as New Zealanders.

But that's not where you find our compelling stories. The things we share are the least interesting things about us. In science as in life, opposites attract. It's tension, pressure, friction and collisions that create energy. It's the same with our culture. What is remarkable about New Zealanders, and what creates the energy within our society is not our sameness; it's the differences between us all.

As the widespread pan-tribal popularity of the street culture that has flowered from the Otara—Cuba Street tribe cross-pollination shows, the more we celebrate our differences and let them rub up against each other, the more vitality and vibrance we create, and the more we like ourselves.

Our contention is that this interaction between the tribes is where the most compelling expressions of the national character of New Zealand are to be found. It's in the interplay between different tribal attitudes going on every day in our homes, our workplaces, our schools, our pubs, on buses and on our sports fields.

There is no typical New Zealander. What is distinctive about us is the sum total of our differences. It's the friction, the antagonism, the understanding and the celebration that goes on between all the 8 Tribes all the time that defines us as New Zealanders.